ISBN 978-0-428-65940-0
PIBN 11301920

NORTHWESTERN UNIVERSITY

EIGHTY-FOURTH
ANNUAL COMMENCEMENT

Saturday, June 13, 1942

FRANCIS JOSEPH HAYDN.
Arranged by P. C. LUTKIN, 1907.

1. Quae-cum-que sunt ve - ra, Pro - ba, jus - ta, me - ra,
2. Ma - ter O be - nig - na, Prae - stans tu - et dig - na

Om - ni - a haec do - na Prae - bes no - bis bo - na
Cus - tos ju - ven - tu - tis, Fi - da dux vir - tu - tis,

Al - ma Ma - ter ca - ra, Ben - e - dic - ta, cla - ra,
Gra - ti - as a - gen - tes, Pi - e re - ve - ren - tes,

Cel - sa in ho - no - re Nos - tro et a - mo - re!
Pen - i - tus a - ma - mus; De - o te man - da - mus. A - men.

J. SCOTT CLARK.

THE COMMENCEMENT

PROCESSIONAL

THE NATIONAL ANTHEM
(The audience will please remain standing until the invocation has been pronounced.)

INVOCATION   THE REVEREND JOHN THOMPSON, D.D.
Pastor Emeritus, First Methodist Church of Chicago

ADDRESS   REAR ADMIRAL WAT TYLER CLUVERIUS, United States Navy (Retired)
President, Worcester Polytechnic Institute

AWARDING OF THE BUREAU OF PERSONNEL NAVAL
R.O.T.C. TROPHY   REAR ADMIRAL JOHN DOWNES, United States Navy
Commandant, Ninth Naval District

AWARDING OF CERTIFICATES

Diploma in Commerce   *Presented by Homer Bews Vanderblue,*
Professor of Business Economics and Dean of the School of Commerce
Diploma as Graduate Nurse   *Presented by Miss Elizabeth Odell,*
Director of the Evanston Hospital School of Nursing
Certificate in Traffic Administration   *Presented by Lieutenant Franklin M. Kreml,*
Director of the Traffic Institute

CONFERRING OF DEGREES IN COURSE

THE COLLEGE OF LIBERAL ARTS   *Presented by Addison Hibbard,*
Professor of English and Dean of the College of Liberal Arts
    Bachelor of Arts with Honors
    Bachelor of Arts
    Bachelor of Science with Honors
    Bachelor of Science

THE SCHOOL OF MEDICINE   *Presented by Dr. J. Roscoe Miller,*
Associate Professor of Medicine and Dean of the School of Medicine
    Doctor of Medicine
    Bachelor of Medicine
    Bachelor of Science in Medicine

THE SCHOOL OF LAW   *Presented by Leon Green,*
Professor of Law and Dean of the School of Law
    Master of Laws
    Juris Doctor
    Bachelor of Laws
    Bachelor of Science in Law

THE SCHOOL OF ENGINEERING   *Presented by Ovid Wallace Eshbach,*
                Dean of the School of Engineering and the Technological Institute
Civil Engineer
Bachelor of Science in Civil Engineering
Bachelor of Science in Electrical Engineering
Bachelor of Science in Industrial Engineering
Bachelor of Science in Mechanical Engineering

THE SCHOOL OF DENTISTRY   *Presented by Dr. Charles W. Freeman,*
                Professor of Oral Surgery and Dean of the School of Dentistry
Master of Science in Dentistry
Doctor of Dental Surgery

THE SCHOOL OF MUSIC   *Presented by John W. Beattie,*
                Professor of Music Education and Dean of the School of Music
Master of Music
Bachelor of Music
Bachelor of Music Education

THE SCHOOL OF COMMERCE   *Presented by Homer Bews Vanderblue,*
                Professor of Business Economics and Dean of the School of Commerce
Master of Business Administration
Bachelor of Science in Commerce

THE SCHOOL OF SPEECH   *Presented by Ralph Dennis,*
                Professor of Literary Interpretation and Public Speaking, and
                Dean of the School of Speech
Bachelor of Science in Speech

THE SCHOOL OF EDUCATION   *Presented by J. Monroe Hughes,*
                Professor of Education and Dean of the School of Education
Master of Science in Education
Bachelor of Science in Education

THE SCHOOL OF JOURNALISM.   *Presented by Kenneth E. Olson,*
                Professor of Journalism and Dean of the School of Journalism
Master of Science in Journalism
Bachelor of Science in Journalism

THE UNIVERSITY COLLEGE   *Presented by Shirley Austin Hamrin,*
                Professor of Education and Director of the University College
Bachelor of Philosophy

THE GRADUATE SCHOOL   *Presented by T. Moody Campbell,*
                Professor of German and Dean of the Graduate School
Master of Arts
Master of Science
Doctor of Philosophy

[6]

CONFERRING OF HONORARY DEGREES

DOCTOR OF SCIENCE—Donald Church Balfour

Professor of Surgery in the Graduate School of the University of Minnesota, Director of the Mayo Foundation for Medical Education and Research, and Head of a Section of Surgery in the Mayo Clinic; honored throughout the world for his accomplishments as a surgeon and for his notable contributions to medical science and education.

Presented by Dr. J. Roscoe Miller, Associate Professor of Medicine and
Dean of the Medical School

DOCTOR OF SACRED THEOLOGY—Wallace Edmonds Conkling

Episcopal Bishop of the Diocese of Chicago; a scholar whose background includes Williams College, the Philadelphia Divinity School, and Oxford University; for eighteen years pastor of one church, during which time both he and the church became nationally known; a wise administrator and spiritual leader; a religious statesman whose influence for good extends far beyond the bounds of his diocese.

Presented by Ernest Lynn Waldorf, Bishop of the Methodist Church
Resident in Chicago

DOCTOR OF FINE ARTS—Carl Milles

Creator of beauty, poet in bronze and marble, teacher of young artists; after a distinguished career in Europe he transferred his skill and loyalty to this western land which he has richly endowed with sculpture and monuments, and where he has lived to exemplify the motto graven over a gate at his home in Sweden: "Let me work while light endures."

Presented by Addison Hibbard, Professor of English and
Dean of the College of Liberal Arts

DOCTOR OF HUMANE LETTERS—William Albert Nitze

A scholar who combines in rare fashion originality and thoroughness in research with brilliance in the presentation of his results; a teacher who has made French literature live in the minds of many generations of American students; a "Distinguished Service Professor" not only in his own University of Chicago but throughout the entire world of higher education.

Presented by T. Moody Campbell, Professor of German and
Dean of the Graduate School

DOCTOR OF SCIENCE—Louis Ernst Schmidt

Scientist, educator, sanitarian, whose noteworthy contributions to the field of public health and the advancement of urological surgery have received world-wide recognition; teacher of great power, whose students have disseminated his idealism widely, assuming the direction of university departments in numerous institutions of higher learning; devoted alumnus of North-western, whose benefactions to the Medical School and to the Archibald Church Library have contributed in generous measure to the steady progress of the University.

Presented by Dr. Irving S. Cutter, Professor of Medicine and
Dean of the Medical School, Emeritus

DOCTOR OF SACRED THEOLOGY—John Thompson

An honored clergyman of the Methodist Church, a pastor of distinguished ability; wise in counsel, sympathetic in ministration, courageous in defending the right and in promoting righteousness; the builder of a stately Temple of Religion in the heart of a great city where his influence will continue and his name will be revered for many years.

*Presented by Thomas F. Holgate, Professor of Mathematics and
Dean of the College of Liberal Arts, Emeritus*

DOCTOR OF SCIENCE—Wat Tyler Cluverius

A creative scientist, president of one of the nation's leading technological institutions, a distinguished officer in the United States Navy, whose brilliant career extended from the sinking of the *Maine* to his retirement in 1939, and who has recently been recalled to active duty in his grade of Rear Admiral; a devoted servant of his country in peace as well as war.

*Presented by Fred D. Fagg, Jr., Professor of Law,
Vice-President and Dean of Faculties*

CHARGE TO THE GRADUATING CLASS   THE PRESIDENT

DELIVERY OF DIPLOMAS

THE UNIVERSITY HYMN   (Words and Music on page 3)

BENEDICTION   THE RIGHT REVEREND WALLACE EDMONDS CONKLING, S.T.D.
The Bishop of Chicago

DEGREES IN COURSE

The appearance of a name on this list is presumptive evidence of graduation but is not to be regarded as conclusive.

DOCTOR OF PHILOSOPHY
With Titles of Dissertations

Joseph Louis Apodaca, B.A., University of Notre Dame, 1930; M.B.A., Northwestern University, 1933. Marketing. *Some Aspects of Advertising and of the Advertisability of Fruits and Vegetables.*

Jerome Walter Archer, B.A., Marquette University, 1930; M.A., 1932. English. *Latin Loan-Words in Early Middle English.*

Donald Herman Atlas, B.S. in Medicine, Northwestern University, 1934; M.S., 1936; M.D., 1938. Medicine. *Studies in Hyperproteinemia.*

George Emerson Beauchamp, A.B., Indiana University, 1928; M.A., University of Michigan, 1930. English. *The Profession of Writing in England 1660-1740.*

William Auburn Behl, A.B., University of South Dakota, 1926; M.A., University of Michigan, 1934. Speech. *The Speaking and Speeches of Theodore Roosevelt.*

Eric John Bradner, B.A., Occidental College, 1928; M.A., Northwestern University, 1931. History. *The Attitude of Illinois Toward Western Expansion in the 1840's.*

Harold Elra Burns, A.B., Oakland City College, 1930; M.A., Indiana University, 1932. Mathematics. *Linear Operators Expressed as Green's Functions with Special Application to the Elastic Plate Problem.*

Joseph Carl Calandra, B.S., Lewis Institute, 1938. Chemistry. *I. Synthesis of Some New Local Anesthetics. II. Carbohydrate Degradation by Sarcinae Luteä.*

Clyde Mevric Campbell, B.S., Knox College, 1924; M.S., University of Illinois, 1933. Education. *Administration of Non-Instructional Activities in Small High Schools.*

Edward Lyle Cooper, B.Ed., State Teachers College, Whitewater, Wisconsin, 1930; M.A., State University of Iowa, 1931. Education. *A Survey of Commercial Education in New York State (excluding New York City) with Implications for the Content of a Fifth Year in the Program of Business Teacher-Education.*

Ernst August Dauer, B.S., Northwestern University, 1929; M.B.A., 1930. Finance. *Comparative Operating Experience of Consumer Instalment Financing Agencies and Commercial Banks, 1929-40.*

Viola Ruth Dunbar, A.B., University of Illinois, 1935; M.A., Northwestern University, 1937. English. *Studies in Satire and Irony in the Works of Henry James.*

Charles Franklin Eckert, B.A., Baker University, 1938. Chemistry. *The Densities of Aqueous Solutions of Certain Electrolytes at 25° C.*

Elwood Henderson Ensor, B.S., Northwestern University, 1938. Chemistry. *Hofmann Degradation Studies Related to Cyclooctatetraene.*

Otis Earl Fancher, B.S., Mississippi State College, 1938. Chemistry. *I. Lactic Acid Production in Carious Lesions. II. Synthesis of Some Alkamine Esters of 4-methoxyisophthalic Acid. III. Synthesis of Some Chloro and Fluoro Amines of the Pressor Type.*

David Martin Fulcomer, B.A., Macalester College, 1932; M.A., University of Minnesota, 1937. Sociology. *The Adjustive Behavior of Some Recently Bereaved Spouses: A Psycho-Sociological Study.*

Sol Louis Garfield, B.S. in Education, Northwestern University, 1938; M.A., 1939. Education. *(Title withheld under agreement with the National Research Council and C.A.A.)*

Kenneth Milton Gordon, A.B., University of Illinois, 1938. Chemistry. *Characterization of Carbohydrates.*

William Claud Henry, B.A., University of Oklahoma, 1936; M.A., 1937. English. *A Study of Alexander Smith and His Reputation as a Spasmodic Writer.*

Frances Rappaport Horwich, Ph.B., University of Chicago, 1929; M.A., Teachers College, Columbia University, 1933. Education. *Parent Education in the Teacher College, and Practice in the Nursery School, Kindergarten and Primary Grades.*

Franklin Weeks Jones, A.B., Harvard University, 1925; M.A., 1927; M.B.A., Northwestern University, 1934. History. *The Origin of the Roman "Delator."*

Saul Kasman, B.S.A.S., Lewis Institute, 1929; M.A., Northwestern University, 1939. Education. *A Comparative Study of the Russian and German Philosophies of Education.*

Samuel Kliger, A.B., University of Michigan, 1931; A.M., 1932. English. *Sir William Temple and the Gothic Cult of the Seventeenth Century.*

Ruth Dorothy Koerber, Diploma, University of Berlin, 1930; M.A., University of Nebraska, 1933. German. *The Authenticity of the "Zeitbilder" in Gutzkow's "Ritter som Geiste."*

Charles Frederick Kremer, Jr., B.S., Northwestern University, 1935; M.A., 1938. English. *Studies in Verse Form in Non-Dramatic English Poetry from Wyatt to Sidney.*

Robert Clarence Kuder, B.A., Ohio State University, 1939. Chemistry. *I. Delphinium Alkaloids. II. Halogenation of 1—Menthone.*

Paul Merville Larson, B.S., Kansas State Teachers College, 1927; M.S., 1929. Speech. *A Rhetorical Study of Bishop Nicholas Frederick Severin Grundtvig.*

Mildred Eunice Manuel, B.S., Beloit College, 1922; M.S., State College of Washington, 1925. Botany. *The Cultivation of Some Unicellular Green Algae.*

Clarence Alva Michelman, B.S., Illinois Wesleyan University, 1925; A.M., University of Illinois, 1935. Education. *A Technique for Classifying Occupations According to the Demands Made on Certain Personal Characteristics of Workers.*

John Preston Moore, B.A., Washington and Lee University, 1927; M.A., Harvard University, 1930. History. *The Colonial Cabildo Under the Spanish Hapsburgs (A Study of the Cabildos of Quito, Santiago (Chile), and Buenos Aires, 1534-1700.)*

Frederick William Mueller, Jr., B.A., University of Minnesota, 1925; M.B.A., Northwestern University, 1933. Finance. *Management of the Earning Asset Portfolios of Forty-One Chicago State Banks.*

Myron Alvin Peyton, A.B., University of Kansas, 1930; M.A., 1931. Spanish. *Don Diego de Noche by Alonso Gerónimo de Salas Barbadillo: A Critical Edition with Introduction and Notes.*

Ralph Frederick Preckel, B.A., Coe College, 1938; M.S., Northwestern University, 1941. Chemistry. *Heats of Dissocation of Some Hexaarylethanes.*

Harold Hunter Scudamore, B.S., Montana State College, 1937; M.S., Northwestern University, 1940. Zoology. *Influence of the Sinus Gland Upon Growth, Molting, and General Metabolism in Crustaceans.*

Lois Kremer Sharpe, B.A., Milwaukee-Downer College, 1927; M.S., University of Rochester, 1932. Geology. *The Paragenesis of Southern Jackson and Macon Counties, North Carolina.*

Frederick George Sherman, B.S., The University of Tulsa, 1938. Zoology. *Density Changes in The Frog's Egg During Normal and Accelerated Development.*

Bain Tate Stewart, B.A., Vanderbilt University, 1936; M.A., 1937. English. *The Renaissance Interpretation of Dreams and Their Use in Elizabethan Drama.*

George William Teuscher, D.D.S., Northwestern University, 1929; M.S.D., 1936; M.A., 1940. Education. *Some Implications of Education and Sociology for Dental Education.*

Edward Julius Thorlakson, B.A., University of Manitoba, 1922; M.A., Northwestern University, 1939. Speech. *The Parliamentary Speaking of Jon Sigurdsson.*

Viola Van Zee, A.B., Pasadena College, 1930; A.M., University of Southern California, 1935. Sociology. *The Role of Recreation in Chicago from 1803 to 1848 as Revealed in Literature Available in the Metropolitan Area.*

Joseph Albert Wells, B.S., University of Denver, 1937; M.S., 1938. Physiology. *The Functional Innervation of the Colon.*

Hilmer Ernest Winberg, B. of Chem., University of Minnesota, 1938. Chemistry. *Condensations Introducing Potential Isoprene Units.*

MASTER OF ARTS

Carrie Marie Anderson, B.S. in Ed., Northwestern University, 1935. Religious Education.

Marjorie Lucille Baumgarten, A.B., Augustana College, 1941. English.

Walter Raymond Beck, B.S. in Ed., DePaul University, 1936. Education.
Louise Petruzzi Bilty, Ph.B., University of Wisconsin, 1929. Education.
Florence Esther Bisbee, A.B., Oberlin College, 1916. Education.
Claire Eva Bornheimer, B.S., Teachers College, Columbia University, 1939. Education.
Kenneth James Bottomley, B.A., Central Y.M.C.A. College, 1938. Education.
David Gilbert Bradley, A.B., University of California, 1938. New Testament.
Gail Soules Bradley, A.B., University of California at Los Angeles, 1940. Systematic Theology.
Louise Braklow, B.A., Iowa State Teachers College, 1928. Education.
Jean Brinig, B.A., College of New Rochelle, 1935. Education.
James Wilson Brock, A.B., Manchester College, 1941. Speech.
Donald Elliott Brown, A.B., North Central College, 1934. Education.
Florencean Bunker, B.S. in Ed., Northwestern University, 1934. English.
Theodora Burch, B.S. in Ed., DePaul University, 1933. Education.
Marion Byrne, B.S. in Ed., Northwestern University, 1940. Education.
Herbert Milton Cadwell, B.S. in Ed., Northwestern University, 1938. Education.
Ada Campbell, B.S. in Ed., Northwestern University, 1940. Education.
Constance Cecilia Campbell, B.A., Mundelein College, 1940. English.
Ruth Campbell, B.S. in Ed., Northwestern University, 1940. Education.
Margaret Converse Carpenter, A.B., Rockford College, 1940. Art.
Margaret Randolph Cason, A.B., Randolph-Macon Woman's College, 1940. English.
Elizabeth Jane Coogan, B.S., Northwestern University, 1941. English.
Howard Freeman Copp, B.S. in Ed., Northwestern University, 1935. Education.
Elizabeth Malley Corey, B.S., Michigan State Normal College, 1938. Education.
Elizabeth Curran, B.A., College of St. Teresa, 1927. Education.
Margaret Elois Davis, B.S. in Home Economics, University of Oklahoma, 1940. Correlated Studies.
Laura Anne Dawson, Ph.B., University of Chicago, 1934. Education.
Charles Otis Decker, B.A., Antioch College, 1941. Education.
Jesse Walter Dees, Jr., A.B., Illinois Wesleyan University, 1936. Sociology.
John Ernest Deiber, B.A., North Central College, 1936. Education.
Helen Celestine DeVault, B.A., Central Y.M.C.A. College, 1939. Education.
Vernell Diefenbronn, A.B., Harris Teachers College, 1931. Education.
Laura Mary Dix, B.S. in Ed., Northwestern University, 1940. Education.
Jacqueline Dombey, B. S. in Ed., Northwestern University, 1941. English.
Arthur Bernard Drought, B.Ed., Milwaukee State Teachers College, 1937. Education.
Elinor Therese Egan, Ph.B., Loyola University, 1938. Education.
Marian Roberta Emerine, B.A., Oberlin College, 1938. Education.
Sophie Laura Fisk, Ph.B., Northwestern University, 1939. French.
Samuel Russel Fouts, B.A., State University of Iowa, 1926. Education.
Margaret Marriner Gallie, B.A., Northwestern University, 1917. Education.
Lois Bagan Galvin, B.S., Northwestern University, 1940. English.
Catherine Fern Garlent, B.A., Albion College, 1934. Education.
Emma Butler Gass, Ph.B., University of Chicago, 1926. Education.
Donna Glyndon, B.Ed., Northern Illinois State Teachers College, 1941. French.
Lillian Weiskopf Gordon, B.S., University of Illinois, 1936. Education.
Lois Bertha Graf, B.A., Clarke College, 1938. Education.
Ethel Jean Graff, B.Ed., National College of Education, 1935. Education.
Edna Ellen Gray, A.B., University of Colorado, 1940. Speech.
Mary Lou Griswold, B.A., Birmingham-Southern College, 1934. Correlated Studies.
Marion Crosley Happ, B.S. in Ed., Northwestern University, 1938. Education.
Frances Marian Harriman, Ph.B. in Ed., University of Chicago, 1931. Education.
Peggy Joan Hausse, B.S. in Ed., Northwestern University, 1941. Spanish.
Myles Frank Havlicek, B.S. in Ed., DePaul University, 1928. Education.
Barbara Alberta Hawkins, B.S. in Ed., Northwestern University, 1934. Education.
Elizabeth Jane Haynes, B.A., Northwestern University, 1941. Latin.

Esther Edith Heyer, Ph.B., Marquette University, 1933. Education.
Mary Louise Hilton, B.A., Northwestern University, 1935. History.
Walter George Hjertstedt, Ph.B., University of Chicago, 1938. Education.
Ben Hoffman, Ph.B., Loyola University, 1938. Correlated Studies.
Ethel Annette Honeycutt, B. Rel. Ed., Woman's Missionary Union Training School, 1931. Correlated Studies.
Beryl Emma Hoyt, A.B., Simpson College, 1936; B.S. in L.S., University of Illinois, 1937. History of Religion.
Lewis Stanley Huber, B.S., University of Illinois, 1927. Education.
Marjorie Estelle Hurwitz, B.E., Northern Illinois State Teachers College, 1939. Education.
Elizabeth Priscilla Jansen, B.S. in Ed., Northwestern University, 1934. Education.
Alma Harrison Jarvis, Ph.B., University of Chicago, 1931. Education.
Kathryn Elizabeth Jasmann, B.A., University of Colorado, 1937. Education.
Theodore H. Jeddeloh, B.E., Illinois State Teachers College, 1939. Education.
Emily Mildred Julian, Ph.B., University of Chicago, 1932. Education.
Norman Kaig, B.A., Central Y.M.C.A. College, 1941. Education.
Charles Kaplan, A.B., University of Chicago, 1940. English.
Kenneth Howard Kaye, B.S., Milwaukee State Teachers College, 1938. Education.
Ralph Waldo Keltner, B.E., Northern Illinois State Teachers College, 1933. Education.
Elmer George Kich, B.S., Capital University, 1923. Education.
Mildred Webster Kirk, B.S. in Ed., Northwestern University, 1935. History.
Nettie Lipman Kramer, B.S. in Ed., Northwestern University, 1935. Correlated Studies.
Adaline Ruth Kroodsma, A.B., Western State Teachers College, 1931. Education.
Winifred Marie Kruzic, B.Ed., Northern Illinois State Teachers College, 1939. Education.
Donald Henry George Kuntz, Ph.B., Marquette University, 1936. Education.
Helen Margaret Kutuzovich, B.A., Northwestern University, 1938. German.
Doris Tomlinson Lackey, B.S. in Ed., Butler University, 1940. Education.
Zenobia Leno Laws, Ph.B., University of Chicago, 1926. Education.
Patricia Churchill Lewis, B.S. in Speech, Northwestern University, 1940. Speech.
Victor Dunleath Lewis, A.B., Fisk University, 1921. Education.
Virginia Frances Lewis, B.S. in Ed., Northwestern University, 1937. Education.
Della Elizabeth Leyse, B.S., Indiana University, 1935. Speech.
June Elizabeth Linderman, B.A., Lawrence College, 1934. Education.
Lilian Vilatzer Liten, B.A., Central Y.M.C.A. College, 1941. English.
Jerome Lathrop Loomis, B.Ed., Whitewater State Teachers College, 1935. History.
Betty C. Love, A.B., State University of Iowa, 1938. Education.
Milton Malkin, B.S.A.S., Lewis Institute, 1940. Education.
William Clifford Manning, B.A., Iowa Wesleyan College, 1939. Ethics.
William Alonzo Martin, A.B., Dartmouth College, 1939. Correlated Studies.
Bertha Elizabeth Martson, B.Ed., Northern Illinois State Teachers College, 1934. Art.
Charles Grieves Mason, A.B., University of Chicago, 1910. Education.
Elizabeth Agnes McCarthy, B.S., Northwestern University, 1917. German.
Leila Allen McMillan, A.B., Ouachita College, 1939. Speech.
Evelyn Peterson Meiners, B. S. in Ed., Northwestern University, 1940. History.
Mollie Caroline Merklein, B.S., Milwaukee State Teachers College, 1938. Education.
Lucy Elizabeth Mildren, A.B., Albion College, 1940. Religious Education.
Clarence Everett Miller, B.S., Northwestern University, 1918. Education.
Leonard W. Miner, B.S., Northwestern University, 1941. Education.
Frank Nelson Moore, S.B., University of Chicago, 1936. Education.
Harry Thornton Moore, Ph.B., University of Chicago, 1934. English.
Alice May Morrill, Ph.B., Denison University, 1917. Education.
Daisy Carter Morton, B.S. in Ed., DePaul University, 1940. Education.
James Myers Mullendore, B.S. in Speech, Northwestern University, 1941. Speech.
Anna Risty Neil, A.B., Augustana College, 1935. Education.
Minnetta Elizabeth Nichols, B.A., Northwestern University, 1941. English.
Marguerite Marie Norre, S.B., University of Chicago, 1934. Education.

Hubert Odishaw, B.A., Northwestern University, 1939. English.
Marcella Pauline Ogurek, B.S. in Ed., University of Nebraska, 1937. Education.
Amy Marguerite Okerlin, B.A., Parsons College, 1929. Education.
Mary Kay O'Malley, B.S. in Ed., DePaul University, 1938. Art.
William Norman O'Neil, B.A., Wiley College, 1927. Education.
James Edwin Orr, Th.B., Northern Baptist Theological Seminary, 1941. Geology, and
    Geography, and History.
Raymond Russell Peters, B.A., Bridgewater College, 1928; B.D., Bethany Biblical
    Seminary, 1936. Religious Education.
Emily A. M. Peterson, B.S. in Ed., Northwestern University, 1937. Education.
Josephine T. Petrus, B.Ed., Chicago Teachers College, 1940. Education.
Hazel Margaret Phillips, Ph.B., University of Chicago, 1928. History.
Michael Pretula, B.S.A.S., Lewis Institute, 1940. Education.
Adele Rabino, LL.B., Northwestern University, 1923; Ph.B., 1937. Correlated Studies.
Robert Charles Rathburn, B.A., Northwestern University, 1941. English.
Monona Evelyn Reeves, B.Ed., Northern Illinois State Teachers College, 1940.
    Education.
Isabelle Hunter Reid, B.S., University of Georgia, 1938. Correlated Studies.
Clara Rebecca Ridgway, B.S. in Ed., California State Teachers College, Pennsylvania,
    1937. Education.
Daniel Johnson Riedel, B.A., Ohio State University, 1933. Correlated Studies.
Tennie Mae.Robinson, A.B., Southwestern University, 1917. Education.
Elfreda Sophia' Romander, A.B., University of California, 1937. Correlated Studies.
Madelyn Rylands, A.B., Drake University, 1934. Education.
James Nathanael Santelle, B.S., Milwaukee State Teachers College, 1938. Education.
Richard Taylor Saunders, Jr., B.S. in Speech, Northwestern University, 1941. Speech.
Geraldine Ione Schafersman, A.B., Midland College, 1939. Speech.
Helen Wheatley Schrader, A.B., Park College, 1936. Speech.
Reuben H. Segel, B.S.A.S., Lewis Institute, 1939. Psychology.
Florence Seidmon, B.S.A.S., Lewis Institute, 1932. Education.
Else Seitzberg, B.S. in Phys. Ed., State University of Iowa, 1930. Education.
Marguerite Nina Shee, B.S. in Ed., Northwestern University, 1939. Education.
Clarence I. Shutes, A.B., University of Michigan, 1916. Education.
Faith Reichelt Smith, B.S., Northwestern University, 1930. Education.
Laura Blandin Smith, B.S. in Ed., Northwestern University, 1938. Education.
Irene Mungovan Spensley, B.Ed., National College of Education, 1937. Education.
Stewart Rowland Spikings, B.S.A.S., Lewis Institute, 1940. Education.
Kathryn Florence Stauder, B.S., University of Illinois, 1931. Education.
Marian Lorraine Stauffer, A.B., University of Illinois, 1940. Spanish.
Annabel Sare Steinhorn, B.A., Northwestern University, 1940. Speech.
Veda Stern, Ph.B.; University of Chicago, 1933' Education.
Margaret Linane Stillman, B.S., DePaul University, 1921. Education.
Bernice Kirkham Terry, B.A., University of Washington, 1922. Education.
Alice Marie Thierman, B.A., Iowa State Teachers College, 1940. History.
Leona Mary Thompson, B.S. in Ed., Northwestern University, 1938. Education.
Carroll Adam Turner, B.Ed., Southern Illinois Normal University, 1939. Education.
Genevieve Joyce Dean Turner, B.A., Beloit College, 1935. Education.
Marjorie Ruth Tweed, B.S. in Ed., Northwestern University, 1940. English.
Lillian Teplitz Udelson, Ph.B., University of Chicago, 1932. Education.
Eilene Weakly, B.A., Northwestern University, 1941. English.
Elizabeth Jean Webb, B.S., Northwestern University, 1939. Education.
Sarah Lillian Webb, A.B., Wesleyan College (Georgia), 1941. Education.
Carl G. Welin, B.S. in Ed., Northwestern University, 1937. Education.
Parsol Merle Wheeler, B.A., Central State Teachers College, 1932. Education.
Alpha Morgan White, A.B., Rust College, 1928. Education.
Jessie Primrose Whyte, A.B., University of Illinois, 1933. Education.

Sallie Irene Wilhelm, B.S. in Ed., Emporia State Teachers College, 1928. Speech.
Robert Henry Wilkerson, B.S., Langston University, 1938. Education.
Helen Wilson Williams, B.A., Wellesley College, 1921. Political Science.
Lola Edith Wilson, A.B., Carleton College, 1926. English.
Harold Martin Wisely, B.A., Stephen F. Austin State Teachers College, 1940. Psychology.
Harriet Christine Wyatt, B.A. in Religion, Furman University, 1936. Education.
Harry M. Zemel, B.A., DePaul University, 1941, History.
Helen Gertrude Zimmerman, B.S. in Ed., Northwestern University, 1938. Education.
Fred William Zirkel, B.Ed., La Crosse State Teachers College, 1929. Education.

MASTER OF SCIENCE

John Morrison Brady, B.S., University of Washington, 1933; B.M., Northwestern University, 1940. Pathology.
Clarence LaRoy Brown, B.A., Valparaiso University, 1939. Geography.
William Adams Bryan, A.B., Princeton University, 1940. Geography.
Weldon Kimball Bullock, B.A., University of Utah, 1930; M.D., Northwestern University, 1934. Pathology.
Dan Youngs Burrill, A.B., University of Michigan, 1929; LLB., 1931; D.D.S., Northwestern University, 1939. Orthodontia.
John Bumpass Calhoun, B.S., University of Virginia, 1939. Zoology.
Dean H. Couch, A.B., Southwestern College, 1940. Chemistry.
Elizabeth Jane Cowgill, A.B., Denison University, 1941. Anatomy.
Jean Bruce Cummings, A.B., Pembroke College, Brown University, 1940. Zoology.
Frank Devlin, A.B., University of Rochester, 1937. Geology.
Alvin Franklin Dodds, B.S., Mississippi State College, 1940. Chemistry.
Donald Huse Dow, B.A., Wesleyan University, 1940. Geology.
Frank Roads Elliott, A.B., Dartmouth College, 1935; M.D., Northwestern University, 1940. Pathology.
Eliot Eugene Foltz, B.S., Northwestern University, 1935; M.D., 1939. Physiology and Pharmacology.
John Otto Gibbs, B.S., Muskingum College, 1936. Pathology.
Franz Rudolf Gotzl, B.S., University of Vienna, 1938. Physiology and Pharmacology.
Victor Hopewell Hough, A.B., Wabash College, 1938. Physiology and Pharmacology.
Deane Frederick Kent, A.B., Middlebury College, 1939. Geology.
George Henry Lowe, Jr., B.S., Northwestern University, 1939. Physiology and Pharmacology.
James Jennings Norton, A.B., Princeton University, 1940. Geology.
John Nurnberger, B.S., Loyola University, 1938. Pathology.
Gaylord Wareham Ojers, B.S., University of Washington, 1937. Physiology and Pharmacology.
Herbert Florian Philipsborn, Jr., B.A., Carleton College, 1937. Physiology and Pharmacology.
Frederick Willard Preston, B.A., Yale University, 1935, M.D., Northwestern University, 1940. Physiology and Pharmacology.
Gustav William Rapp, B.S.A.S., Lewis Institute, 1940. Chemistry.
Robert Allen Roback, A.B., University of California, 1941. Physiology and Pharmacology.
Wesley Fitch Roberts, A.B., Brown University, 1939. Zoology.
Eugene Rex Schleiger, B.A., Hastings College, 1940. Physics.
David Shapiro, A.B., New York University, 1941. Zoology.
Mortimer Hay Staatz, B.S., California Institute of Technology, 1940. Geology.
Richard Harlan Stark, A.B., University of Kansas, 1938. Mathematics.
Dorothy Peterson Stoner, A.B., University of Nebraska, 1926. Biology.
Kermit Briggs Streeter, A.B., Colgate University, 1940. Chemistry.
Arnold Louis Wagner, B.S., Northwestern University, 1936. Medicine.
Ralph Henry Wilpolt, B.A., Lawrence College, 1940. Geology.

James Clinton Winters, B.A, University of Wichita, 1939. Chemistry.
Richard Dawson Wood, B.S. in Ed., Ohio State University, 1940. Botany.
Leona Brandes Yeager, B.A., North Central College, 1929. Bacteriology.

BACHELOR OF ARTS WITH HONORS

Dorothy Harriet Aldridge
†Kenneth Charles Cleophas
†Margaret Helen Cox
Mary Jane Fetzer
Marvin Fox
†Seymour Abraham Fox
Fay Bettye Goldman
Mary Ruth Latenser

‡Randolph Walke McCandlish, Jr.
Louise Eleanor Menning
Marjorie Louise Minster
†Claire Joseph Raeth
†Earl Robert Schwass
Virginia Annabelle Wack
†Frances Webb
Frank Myron Wright, Jr.

BACHELOR OF ARTS

Leila Jane Abrahams
Jean Bundy Boggs
Robert Crown
Robert Bruce Holmgren
Betty Jane Homer
Louise Carrol Hoy
Robert Lourie Larson
Italia Frances Malato
Carolyn Greenwood McManis
Renée Dorothy Mendelsohn

Leonard Murphy
Dorothy Olive Owen
Ruth Elizabeth Plass
Henry Karl Puharich
Herbert Raffeld
Robert John Salvesen
Donald Murray Smith
Laura June Smith
Betty Corinne Smothers
Harriett Kathryn Wolfe

BACHELOR OF SCIENCE WITH HONORS

Norman Carl Anderson
John Corby Andrae
‡Edna Elizabeth Ash
Betty Waterman Bader
Edwin Renken Blomquist
Ruth Brenner
Lucille Frances Brotman
‡Elizabeth Wilbourn Cobb
Katharine Frances Crofts
James Henry Eldredge, Jr.
Fremont Chandler Fletcher
‡Phyllis May Ford
Maxine Louise Gordon
Joseph Palmer Graf
Seymour Greenberg
Carl David Guldager
Virginia Ann Gum
Jean Ellen Harper
Clifford Byron Hicks
Max Lorraine Hillmer, Jr.
†Dorothy Jane Kell
Alice Raymer Kimbell

Russell Vernon Kohr
†Lois Helen La Croix
‡Gordon Elleroy Langlois
Ruth Lichthardt
†Portia Osie McClain
Bruce Hiram Millen
Mary Ellen Munger
†Alice Elizabeth Nightingale
Florence Louise Owen
Richard Leonard Park
‡Walter Shoemaker Phares
†Catherine Barbara Putnik
†Bernard Gordon Rosenthal
†Mary Ellen Sams
†Herbert Steinberger
†Yale Jerome Topper
James Robertson Ward
†Jean Louise Weiss
Virginia Ruth Wells
†Jack Palmer White
†Harry Bixler Williams, Jr.

‡*With Highest Distinction.*
†*With Distinction.*

BACHELOR OF SCIENCE

Ada Abromowitz
William Kemp Absher
Bernard Henry Adelson
Ann Carolyn Albers
Jerome David Albert
Jean Magdalene Alessi
Bernard Marshall Alter
Gordon Caldwell Anderson
Herbert William Anderson, Jr.
James Robert Anderson
Margaret Lucille Anderson
Winnifred Anderson
William Fuller Arendt
Alfred Sampson Arnott
Mary Elizabeth Arns
Howard Arvey
William George Bagnuolo
Samuel Jerry Baim
Betty Bell Baker
John Robert Ballenger
Richard Read Barber
George Robert Bartron
Elizabeth Baumann
Robert Edward Bedessem
Phyllis Below
Dorothy Marcia Bennett
Tibey Mildred Berman
Eldrid Martha Bernts
Guy Neill Berry II
Billie Delores Bichacoff
Leo Bird, Jr.
Beryl Alan Birndorf
Doris Marjorie Black
Ruth Elizabeth Black
Peter Arild Blichert
Mary Christine Blomgren
Lois Wilma Boon
Eloise Meta Boone
Constance Kemp Booth
Clark Henry Boren
Helen Bric
Ann Elizabeth Bricker
Evelyn Dorothea Broder
Robert Louis Brookman
Virginia Florence Buhrke
Nita Sara Burack
Merle Stephen Burdick
Ethel May Burkholder
Donald Owen Burst
Betty Jo Byersdorf
George Loring Carlson
Richard Wallace Carlson
Robert Cooke Carmody
Wallace Taylor Carr
Eleanor Chamberlain
Marie Odile Chamberlain

Ralph Emerson Clarke
William Ellis Coates
Patricia Coatsworth
Beverly Coffman
Paul Curt Cohen
Helen Grace Collins
Leon Spencer Cook
Margaret Mary Cornet
Virginia Marshall Coyner
Barbara Louise Cramer
Ruth Eleanor Cullis
William Emery Cunningham
Jane Lee Davis
John DeLee Degenhardt
Edward Joseph Detmer
Jeanne Bennett Devereaux
Walter Harlan Dey
Virginia Adele Dick
Charles Robert Dickinson
Jane Louise Diller
Ruth Marie Dillon
Marjorie Dimpelfeld
Pearl Violet Dittman
Fred E. Dohrs
Raymond Bancroft Domoney
Patrice Elizabeth Duncan
Kathryn Isabelle Dunlay
Alexandru Gheorghe Edeleanu
Howard Milton Edwards, Jr.
June Alice Edwards
Gregory Joseph Egan
Jacques Friedland Ehle
Esadora Evalyn Elbaum
Robert Whitcomb Ellingwood
Robert McClure Ellis
Marion Wilson Emerson
Vera Engblom
Richard Alfred Erdlitz
Mary Frances Faulkner
Charles Mathew Feingarten
Martha Louise Fidler
Lee Earle Fischer
Wesley Robert Fishel
Mary Jane Fisher
Patricia Marie Fisher
Marjorie Frank
Don Abell Frantz
Eileen Francis Frawley
Beverly Ann Friedman
Dorothy Jean Fuller
Jacques Graydon Fuller
Leonard William Gabris
Margaret Eugenia Gallagher
Phyllis Elizabeth Galvin
Phil Horton Gardner, Jr.

John Preston Garriott
Miriam Betty Gevirman
Robert Philip Gildred
Miriam Glabman
Joleen Blanche Glassner
James Douglas Goddard
Francis Xavier Golniewicz, Jr.
Haskell Howard Gordon
Rosalie Webb Gosselin
Janet Eloise Grede
Richard Louis Greiner
Edith Delight Gressley
Helen Jane Grieve
George Walter Grill, Jr.
Bernice Lorraine Gross
Edythe Frances Gross
Patricia Jean Grover
Ruth Lorraine Guthrie
Frank Haldane Haigler, Jr.
Frank Richard Hall
David Edwin Hallstrand
Gertrude Elizabeth Halstead
Edgar Simon Hammerberg
Alice Jane Hanson
David Michael Hardy
Charlotte Beatrice Harris
Esther Betty Harris
Rosalind Strawn Hartshorn
Hertha Louise Hartung
Eleanor Naomi Hassmann
Eleanor Wyne Hatfield
Cyril Henry Hauser
Lois Kristin Hellstrom
Margaret Dorothy Hempel
Graham Elden Heniken
Ruth Ashworth Heywood
Carson Parks Higgins
Margery Anita Hixon
Joseph Albert Hollander, Jr.
John Todd Holmes, Jr.
Nelda Bastiani Holmgren
Harwood Hoover
Harriet Horwich
Carl Arthur Hotze
Margaret Pope Hovey
Norma·Helen Hubrig
Margaret Ann Hudson
Dorothy Page Huff
Marijane Hurja
Margaret Hurtz
Charles Selwyn Jackson
Marion Katherine Jacobs
John Frederic Johnson
Muriel May Johnson
Mary Helen Johnston
Katherine Alice Jones
Vern Allen Jones
Norma Ruth Jordan

Bernard Joseph
Marjorie Ruth Juergens
Jacqueline Kadet
James Peter Frank Kakarakis
Joel Katz
Jessie Jean Kelly
Hall Ketchum
Florence Frances Ketchoo
Charlotte Kieferstein
Patricia King
Clyde August Kirchhoff
Robert William Kittredge
Elwin Merrick Kleihauer
  (as of the class of 1939)
Eileen Elise Kollman
Roy Joseph Korn
Gerald David Kupper
Constantine Peter Kutrumanes
Alice Bertha La Buy
Pritchard Ting Chew Lam
Beverly June Lambert
Jean Hruby Langworthy
Margaret Jane Lawler
John Martin Lee
Barbara Jane Lefler
Mary Eleanor Lemke
George Harold Lichtenstein
Ralph Theodore Lidge
Ruth Katherine Lieber
Jack Ellis Liebling
David Albert Lindsey
Ruth Ann Lipsker
Earl Harris Mabry
Lorna Jean MacCallum
Marie Anna Mack
Frances Magisano
Florence Lillian Magnuson
Gabrielle Catherine Mantz
Carline Margolis
Louise Virginia Marsh
Jeanne Marshall
Elizabeth Holmes Mathews
Eloise McCann
Freeman McCann
Lawrence John McCormack
Helen Grace McCullough
John Ralph McDermott
Claude Victor Meconis
John Francis Meeth
Gloria Meiselman
Mary Sena Meister
David Henry Melbye
Margaret Bernece Mengel
Gayle Evelyn Menk
Mary Dawn Mettome
Cynthia Jane Meyer

Garfield Frederick Miller, Jr.
Theodore White Miller
Robert Mills
Nicholas William Moreth
George Eldred Morgan
Dorothy Elsa Morosnick
Marilynn Marjory Mose
Helen Edith Moss
Harold Nadler
Norma Nevah Nicholson.
Virginia Elizabeth Nickel
Mary Proudfit Noble
Vivian Noskin
Frank John Novak III
Pauline Jane Nutt
Mary Avery Ogden
Betty Ann Olson
Donald Albert Olson
Nancy Keen Olson
Ralph Gordon Orr
Elizabeth Jean Ottenheimer
William Marriott Otto
Dorothy Adelaide Padden
Janice Arminta Parker
William Gordon Paullin
Arthur Morris Pearson
Victor Samuel Peters
Martin Albert Pfotenhauer II
Dorris Pearl Pike
Margaret Henderson Platt
Helen Chamberlain Poor
Mary Jane Poranski
Diana Porikos
George William Putnam, Jr.
Hope Lorraine Quirk
Lon Willing Ramsey
Barbara Ramseyer
Marjorie Elsie Rogers
Blanche Rosen
Cecile Rosen
Evelyn Rosen
Leon DeLee Rosenfeld
Jean Dorothy Ross
Frances Ross-Shannon
Josephine Merriella Roth·
Patricia Hamilton Rowntree
Emilie Marie Rozumski
Dorothy Rubin
Janet Sampson
Jack Gustav Schafer
Jane Elizabeth Schram
Joseph Benson Schrock
Dorothy May Schultz
Maynard Arthur Schwerdlin

Helen Schwoeffermann
Frances Coe Sesler
Ade Louis Shaw, Jr.
Carl William Simonson
Opal Mercedes Smerchek
Charlotte LaRue Smith
Florence Evelyn Smith
Marcia Hurn Smith
Helen Virginia Sober
Wallace George Solum
Hazel Wilton Southgate
Ruth Mary Sprenger
Hugo Stange
Vivian Marie Stange
Mavis Earlene Starr
Elaine Adele Stechbart
Irving Stemerman
Glenn Charles Stock
Richard Charles Strasser
Mary Louise Stratton
John Murray Strittar
Elizabeth Alice Strong
John Rogers Sundine
Jules Francis Szatkowski
Theodore William Taub
Mary Ellen Thompson
Norma Jean Thulin
Sheila Anne Treis
Richard Arnold Trubey
Claude Udkoff
Betty Joan Ullrich
Virginia May Vojtech
Warren Russell Von Ehren
Virginia Kennelly Walters
Donald Butler Ward, Jr.
William John Warmington
Hugh Robert Waters
Theodore Francis Weber
Herbert Weinstein
John Bernard Welsh
Robert Warren Wencil
Dawn Thompson Weston
Jane Alice Whike
Elizabeth Grace White
Helen Whyte
Mel Edna Wiechert
Edith Emma Wiesen
Margaret Ruth Williams
Meyer Williams
Ervin Fillmore Wilson
Prentice Henry Eugene
  Winfield, Jr.
Rae Gabriel Winter
Helen Grace Winters
Edward Martin Wones, Jr.

Walter Maurice Woolfson, Jr.
Jean Craig Woolhiser
Marcelle Pearl Worel ·
Marian June Young

Earl Zazove
Helen Ruth Zeman
Anne Catherine Zimmer
Marvin Charles Ziporyn

DOCTOR OF MEDICINE

Theodore Orestes Alexander
Theodore Edwin Alm
Alfons Ralph Altenberg
Charles Edward Baker
Frederick Greiner Barr, Jr.
Robert Gilmore Barrick
Clyde Gordon Bassett
Morrison Douglas Beers
Alvin Leo Berman
George Jaeger Best
Paul Frederick Betzold
Henry J. Bjorge
Henry Bernard Blumberg
Ernest Rittenhouse Bowman
Robert Nelson Bridenbaugh
George Junior Bulkley
Leo Marshall Columbus
Paul Marvin Consigny
Robert Dean Cook
Harney May Cordua, Jr.
Charles Kermit Dilley
Frank Robert Dutra
Millard Henry Duxbury
Leonard Anthony Dwinnell
Morton Howard Fingerhut
Forrest Llewellyn Flashman
George Christian Frederickson
John Victor Freestone
Robert Trumanne Gardner
James Gustave Golseth
David Gomberg
Kenneth Grant
Thomas James Gray
Durward Belmont Greer, Jr.
Donald Eccles Hansen
Robert Rogers Harriage
Waldo Evan Harris
Stearley Pike Harrison
Weston Ackland Heinrich
Howard Wyatt Heywood
Charles Van Kirk Hillman, Jr.
Fred Weber Holmes
Winthrope R. Hubler
Daniel Robert Kohli
Frederick William Kraft
Robert E. Lane
Rudolph Robert Lang

William Alexander Larmon
Claude Stanley Larson
Claude Wilson Lavender
Gwilym Bowen Lewis
Wilbur Sayre Lummis, Jr.
John Thomas Manwaring
William Henry Marlowe
Janet Ward McArthur
Charles Berkeley McIntosh
Kilian H. Meyer
A. Watson Miller
Richard Ward Mills, Jr.
Robert A. Moore ·
Jack Tullus Murphy
Richard Montgomery Oliver
Edwin Robert Orr
Richard Edward Orr
John Thomas Parker
Ben Miller Peckham
Brendan Pearse Phibbs
Gordon Woodrow Raleigh
Henry David Rees
Martin Joseph Reimringer
James Whitcomb Riley
Richard Arlos Rink
Ausey Hamilton Robnett
Caroline Elizabeth Rockwell
James Del Rogers
Robert Smedley Rothwell
Rufus Capers Rucker
Freeman Lester Sampson
Earl Boyce Sanborn
Louis Sarro
Alfred Max Slotta
Burton Jacob Soboroff
William Frank Steuber
Edward Thomas
Edmund Howard Torkelson
George Norman Vigeland
Robert Moore Waters
Charles Matthew Webster
Bernard Joseph Weinberg
William Charles Westen
Harold Ward Wick
Audrey Lagerquist Wilson
Edward Thomas Wilson
Kane Zelle

BACHELOR OF MEDICINE

Jean Jacobus Austin
Donald Church Balfour, Jr.
Douglas Claude Barker
David Ritch Barnum
Harry Jacobs Bartron, Jr.
Howard G. Bayley, Jr.
Wilford Gwilliam Biesinger
Robert Blatherwick
Edward Clyde Bobb
Jean Alphonse Bourdeau
John Newton Briggs
Emil Wilson Brooking
Wilford Armond Brooksby
Edwin Carl Burklund
James McKenzie Catlin
George Herman Cech
Edward Joseph Chereck
Fred Gillett Cox
Delos Robert Cozad
Howard Whitfield Crail
William Purdie Daines
†Edward Henry Daseler
Leo Walter Doyle, Jr.
Joseph Erhart Fischnaller
†John Davidson Frame, Jr.
Sanford Robinson Gifford, Jr.
Harry Bennett Gilbert
William Thiesen Graham
Harry England Grant
Albert Crow Hatcher
Edgar Frank Heiskell, Jr.
Ferris Dean Highsmith
Walter Ernest Hinz
Charles Elwin Hughes
Edward Jozaitis
Earl Lennox Keyser
Herbert Hale Kilgore
Roland Paul Ladenson
Alvin Ruben Larson
George Henry Lowe, Jr.
Paul Henry Luft
Anibal Lugo Lugo

Almon Augustus Manson
Edward Franklin Mee
Harold A. Mermelstein
Lawrence Edward Metcalf
Jack Metcoff
George Edward Miller
†Edward Henry Morgan
Kenneth Lyle Morris
Reinard Peter Nanzig
Clarence Arthur Norberg
Carl Oscar Nord
Gaylord Wareham Ojers
William Howe Otis
Frank Thomas Padberg
Robert Henry Pfeifer
Herbert Florian Philipsborn, Jr.
Roger Kenneth Phillips
Harrison C. Putman, Jr.
Milton Dunne Ratner
Alice Josephine Richardson
Robert Leary Rood
Russell C. Rowan
Lloyd Odus Rupe
Theodore Herbert Sattler
Jack Junior Saxe
John Christian Seidensticker
George Arthur Shawkey
†Alfred Irvin Shopera
George Donald Shull
Marvin Walter Simmons
Carroll H. Smith, Jr.
Philip W. Smith
John Howard Sterne
Robert Frank Swanson
Pierce William Theobald
Henning Harper Thorpe
John Warkentin
Jay Justin Welch
Robert Thatcher Wheeler
Carter Henry Wieneke
Fredric William Wilson
MacDonald Wood

BACHELOR OF SCIENCE IN MEDICINE

George Constantine Anison
Earl Lawrence Barrett
Carl Bennett Bean
John Louis Bell
Robert Vincent Bourdeau
Joseph Thane Chung
Paul L. Conrad
Gordon O. Erlandson
Edward David Fikany
LeRoy John Fox

Donald Robert Hammond
Warren Grant Harlan
Lucius Clark Hollister, Jr.
Paul Gerry Kliewer
Warren John Kraft
Frederic Allen Lestina
Roderick Hugh Maguire
Russell Meadows, Jr.
H. Ross Merrill
Gene Hanford Parsons

†*With Distinction.*

[20]

Matthew Moss Patton
James Haddon Allen Peck, Jr.
Charles D. Rehm
Charles Augustus Short, Jr.

LaVern Lake Swigart
Francis Aldis Torrey
Jack Welby Weidner
Frederick Morris Zundel

MASTER OF LAWS

Jacob Joseph Gordon

JURIS DOCTOR

Raymond William Ashton
William René Bugé
Howard P. Castle
Raymond Orion Clutter
Robert Kane Dower
John William Dubbs, Jr.
Milton Fields
Stanley Benjamin Frosh
J. Edward Goggin
William Daniel Good
David McDonald Gooder
Robert Tsonhyuin Huang

Walker Allen Jensen
Stephen Edward Ladd
Theodore Peter Lambros
Amy Ruth Mahin
James Andrew Rahl
Marshall David Sampson
Joseph George Solari
John Wellington Stewart
John Montague Teevan
Thomas Goodman Vent, Jr.
Joseph Anton Zygmuntowicz

BACHELOR OF LAWS

Joseph Albaum
Joseph Allan Dubbs
Kenneth Lloyd Hecht
Marvin Lee Koenigsberg
Sherwin Robert Rodgers

Benjamin Rosengard
Homer Stanley Rosenthal
Jerome Silberg
David Wandell

BACHELOR OF SCIENCE IN LAW

Byron Hill Beaton
Alexandre Paul Boisdeau
John Robert Broadway
Kirkpatrick Wallwick Dilling
Jacob Louis Frank
Marvin Lee Koenigsberg
Warren Krinsky
Arthur Quentin Larson, Jr.
Alfred Wall Lewis, Jr.

Morton D. Lieberman
Ferdinand Benjamin Peik, Jr.
John Gordon Poust
G. Wallace Roth
Walter Peter Steffen
Robert L. Tarrel
William Powell Treacy
David Wandell

CIVIL ENGINEER

John C. Sanderson, Jr., B.S., Northwestern University, 1932. *Construction of the Northwestern Technological Institute Building,*

BACHELOR OF SCIENCE IN CIVIL ENGINEERING

Chester Henry Cole
Robert Franklin Edbrooke
William Robert King

Joseph Eugene Love, Jr.
Edward Martin McMillan
George Boris Nicoloff

BACHELOR OF SCIENCE IN ELECTRICAL ENGINEERING

George Weldon Carlson
Robert Augustus Derrickson
Eugene George Key

Isadore Kraitsik
Marvin Alfred Kruse
Gegory Theodore McLean

[21]

James Herbert Pomerene
David Lewis Ringwalt
Geoffrey James Robinson
Stephen Philip Ronzheimer

John Schmidt, Jr.
Aubrey Arthur Smith
Martell Freeman Tuntland

BACHELOR OF SCIENCE IN INDUSTRIAL ENGINEERING

Eugene Price Brown, Jr.
Richard Louis Fahrbach
Wallace Reid Giedt
Robert John Lee

Edgar Huston Olds
Lucien Gianella Osborne
Christian Henry Petersen, Jr.

BACHELOR OF SCIENCE IN MECHANICAL ENGINEERING

Harry Elton Albright
Sidney Eaton Bates, Jr.
Hans Gram Bechmann
  Birnbaum
Robert Carl Boehm
William Harrison Coulter
Paul Glenn Feld
Charles George Filstead, Jr.

Paul Nicholas Garay
Francis Elliott Healy
Dugald C. Jackson III
Rossall James Johnson
Stanley Joseph Skaistis
Leonard Vincent Sloma
Clarence Earle Spanjer
Layman John Wilkinson

MASTER OF SCIENCE IN DENTISTRY

With Titles of Theses

Fred Austin Boyd, D.D.S., Loyola University School of Dentistry, New Orleans, Louisiana, 1939. *The Early Reactions of the Adjacent and Supportive Dental Tissues to the Application of Orthodontic Ligatures.*

DaCosta Clark, D.M.D., North Pacific College of Oregon, 1934. *A Clinical Study of Local Implantation of Sulfonamide Compounds in Oral Surgical Wounds.*

Clifton Orrin Dummett, B.S., Central Y.M.C.A. College, 1941, D.D.S., Northwestern University, 1941. *A Study of the Frequency of Gingival Inflammation and Gingival Crevices with Relation to Type and Age of Teeth in Human Beings.*

Robert Winlock Dunn, D.D.S., University of Illinois, 1921. *A Clinical Study of the Results of Various Post-Operative Treatment of Extraction Wounds.*

Joseph George Fishbein, B.S., Rhode Island State College, 1937, D.D.S., Temple University, 1941. *A Clinical and Radiographic Study of the Use of Synthetic Bone Paste in Root Resection Crypts.*

Jerome Fleeman, D.D.S., Northwestern University, 1941. *A Study of the Osteology of the Guinea Pig Skull.*

Ivor Eric Godfrey Hunter, L.D.S., University of Liverpool, England, 1926. *An Investigation of the Efficiency of Model Investments.*

Charles S. Kresnoff, B.S.D., D.D.S., Northwestern University, 1936. *Investigation of the Use of Occipital Anchorage in Orthodontic Treatment.*

Takashi Mayeda, D.D.S., Northwestern University, 1941. *Effects of the Various Types and Shapes of Wrought Iridio-Platinum Reinforcements upon the Physical Properties of Dental Porcelain.*

John C. McGuire, Jr., D.D.S., Northwestern University, 1940. *A Study of the Eruption Pattern in Orthodontic Patients Between the Ages of Six and Twelve Years.*

Adrian LeRoy Swanson, D.D.S., Northwestern University, 1940. *Phosphatase Content of Healing Alveolar Bone.*

Jean-Paul Trottier, B.A., Seminaire de Nicolet, 1936, D.D.S., University of Montreal, 1941. *A Study of Processing Strains in Acrylic Resins.*

Edwin Linn Young, B.S., University of Dayton, 1939, D.D.S., Northwestern University, 1941. *A Clinical Study to Determine Comparative Anesthetic Efficiency of Procaine Hydrochloride at Various pH Levels.*

DOCTOR OF DENTAL SURGERY

John A. Anderson
Peter Warren Appel
Thomas Harper Armstrong
Melvin Barnett
Alberto Barriga Giordano
Kurt James Baum
Glenn E. Boring, Jr.
William John Brockington
Lorenz Pope Bunker
John Joseph Byrnes
Thomas Mosgrove Campbell
Theodore Franklin Carter
Jack LeRoy Coleman
Harris Rogers Cox
Robert James Curley
Loren William Curtis
James Blaine Dickenson, Jr.
Walter Bruce Doering
Alex Fox
Marcus C. Funk
Harold Leon Galvin
Arthur Harold Gilbert
Thomas Edward Gilmore, Jr.
Arthur Eugene Gunderson
Dave Crosby Gunter
Herbert Carl Gustavson
George Nelson Hartley
Scott Bernard Harvey
Rudolf Hecht
Leslie James Helbing
Robert David Henry
Frederic Samuel Hill

Edward S. Holman
Roland Vater Houck
John Ide Ingle
Cheddi Jagan
Charles Cordell Jarrett
James Henry Kalk
Lawrence Glenn Khedroo
John Anton Kollar, Jr.
Ricardo Kriebel Rodriguez
Thomas Edmund Lewis
Clifford Kaye Lossman
Warren Robert Mayne
Elmus E. Miles
Seymour Fred Miller
Stanley Susumu Miyakawa
Raymond Gregory Orsinger
Harold Burton Pattishall, Jr.
Robert B. Petraitis
Ludwell Cowan Pierce
Frank A. Rago
Emil F. Riha
Stanley W. Riha
Gösta Rydberg
Donald Keith Sargent
Robert Rodolphe Schroeder
Frank Wells Sproul, Jr.
Robert Curvin Strayer
Walter Louis Valentinas
S. E. Reyes Veglio
Harry F. Wade
Morris Jay Warburton

DENTAL HYGIENISTS

Betty Lou Burns
Frances Lisbeth Dorsey
Shirley Erstling
Dorothy Henneges

Jean Kleiman
Mary Alice Mayne
Irene Resnick
Carol Anne Yarmey

MASTER OF MUSIC

Inez Leone Archer
Charles Edgar Baker
Noyes Nathan Bartholomew
Evalene Jane Bell
Edward Gardner Benedict
Earl Raymond Bigelow
Vivian Josephine Coghlan
John Walker Creighton
Barbara Davis
Fred Edward Dempster
William Alfred Eberl
Ruth Adelaide Ecton
Theodore Frederick Eichler
Helen Eichhorn Fulghum
Mary Matilda Gaume

David Frederick Geppert
Gordon Oliver Gilbertson
Helen Emily Gipson
Milton Goldberg
Dorthea Maxine Gore
Mary Louise Gray
Marguerite Kolberg Hall
Sherwood Estabrook Hall
William Vernal Hankins
Phyllis Fergus Henderson
Barbara Richmond Holt
Harry Marvin Jacobs
Marguerite Ann Kelly
Corinne Minna Kerner
Ira Aaron Kipnis

[23]

Frank Kratky
Stanley Stewart Linton
Marian Louise Loveless
Ethyl May MacDonald
Richard Vickrey Madden
David Moll
Lloyd Bernard Norlin
Henry Thompson Paine
Dorothy Alice Palmer
Bertha Josephine Parker
Ralph Cloyd Riffe
Nelmatilda Landers Ritchie
George Russell Ross

Orvin Anvenis Sale
Ernst Sigvard Sanderson
Alice Louise Slocomb
John Walter Lawrence Stilley
Dorothy Lynn Taylor Stratton
John Carl Tegnell
Claire Adrienne VanderGriend
Sylvesta Marie Wassum
Minnie Dee Weaver
Eloise Willis
Clayton Herbert Wilson
Mary Louise Wood
Lavina Zabel

BACHELOR OF MUSIC

Peter Hooper Alderwick
Reba Mae Burrows
Anna-Louise deRamus
Frederick Cunningham Elbel
Rose Mary Green
John Thomas Haskell
Genevieve Geraldine Hresiokt
Evonne Therese Jacquart
Patricia Irene Jillson
Albert Richard Johnston

Arlene Marion Fromm Koenig
Anthony DeWild Kooiker
Frances Mary Maraldo
Kathryn Elizabeth McDonald
Anne Clark Ogden
Frances Cottrell Pryor
Amanda Vick Robbins
Susan Marion Seale
Lydia Florence Smithmeyer
Carolyn Lynn Westbrooke

BACHELOR OF MUSIC EDUCATION

Betty Jean Alexander
Anna Rose Balistreri
Clifford George Benson
Roswell Gordon Coburn
Elizabeth Dyer Coles
Daisy May Hughes D'Ambrosio
Judy Marie Denney
Dorothy Ellen Feemster
Mary Ruth Fleming
Ann Lee Gibas
Ellen Gertrude Greenberg
Evelyn Ross Greene
Leon Hirsh Guide
Alma Lavinia Hall
Wilma Jane Hare
Lois Virginia Harper
Jane Boydstun Hay
Claribel Hill
Harriet Jeanne Hoettchen
Bernice Emilia Hornig
Genevieve Geraldine Hresiokt
Jeannette Sykes Jensen
Reuben John Johnson
Robert Vincent Jones
Eugene Harrow Keck
Charlotte Jane Kickhaefer

Patricia Marie King
Eleanore Lanz
Joseph Stanley Leach
Edna Sophia Mack
Jeanne Elizabeth McClayton
Betty Jane Neis
Margaret Vaughan Norris
William John Peterman
Elaine Jean Poltrock
Valentine Preston
James Munro Riewer
Shirley Dolores Rotstein
Bernadine Saltz
Arwin Jack Schweig
Elizabeth Kathryn Smith
Hertha Marie Staehelin
Allan Stahl
Lavern Alvin Stassen
Newton Dwight Strandberg
Mary Jane Ten Eyck
Gordon Bertrand Terwilliger
Eleonora Joan Toldo
Martha Marian Veysey
Edith Mann Vivian
Elaine Cordelia Wright
Irving Malcolm Zeller

MASTER OF BUSINESS ADMINISTRATION
With Titles of Theses

Donald Campbell Brabston, A.B., Birmingham-Southern College, 1941. *Accounting Treatment for Goodwill.*

Anthony Elmo Cascino, B.S., Lewis Institute, 1939. *A Development of the Secular Trend of Railway Freight Traffic of Agricultural, Animal, and Forest Products, 1919 to 1942.*

William Gene Chappell, B.S. in B.A., Bowling Green State University, 1940.

Frank John Charvat, B.S., University of Illinois, 1937. *Financial Analysis of Class I Motor Carriers of Property.*

Lilburn Carl Clark, Jr., B.S. in B.A., University of Tulsa, 1940.

Clyde Clinton Cleveland, B.A., Emmanuel. Missionary College, 1936. *Financial Budgetary Control and Managerial Accounting Reports for Seventh-Day Adventist Academies and Colleges.*

Mildred Jean Crites, B.A., University of Oregon, 1941.

Mortimer Adolph Dittenhofer, B.A., Macalester College, 1937. *The Application of a Punch Card System to a Representative Firm in the Restaurant Supply Industry.*

Joe Perry Dyer, B.S., University of Utah, 1940.

Wayne Walter Gross, B.S. in Com., Northwestern University, 1941.

Luther Andrews Henderson, B.S. in Com., Texas Christian University, 1941. *An Accounting System for Small Southern Lumber Mills.*

Katherine Vakos Kissel, B.A., University of Wisconsin, 1938.

Lewis Carl Mathews, B.S., Nebraska State Teachers College, 1941.

Hugh John May, B.S. in Com., Northwestern University, 1941.

Mary Jean McFadden, B.S., University of North Dakota, 1940.

John Ross Meredith, B.A., University of British Columbia, 1939. *The Investment Characteristics of Petroleum Bonds.*

William Oliver, B.S.C., Southern Methodist University, 1941. *The Accounting System of a Fire Insurance Company.*

Paul Pike Pullen, B.A., University of Wisconsin, 1912. *Population Movements in the Chicago Area from 1900 to the Present.*

Harold Charles Refling, B.A., St. Olaf College, 1941. *A Study of a Rural North Dakota Bank.*

Rafael Fabregas Romaguera, B.B.A., University of Puerto Rico, 1941. *Accounting Treatment of Contingency Reserves.*

Frances Allene Smith, B.S., University of Alabama, 1941. *The Psychological Impact of Bar Soap Advertising—Based on a Survey of 445 Women in Evanston, Illinois.*

James Stewart Wilson, B.S. in Com., Northwestern University, 1931. *Accounting for Soy Bean Operations as Illustrated by Procedures of Acme Soy Bean Products Company.*

John Myron Witte, B.A., University of Wisconsin, 1940.

Charles Edward Wolff, B.S., Lewis Institute, 1937. *A Study of Shopping Newspapers in Forty Cities in the United States.*

BACHELOR OF SCIENCE IN COMMERCE

Paul Arnold Abrahamson, Jr.	Mansfield Homer Beatty, Jr.
Arnold Abrams, Jr.	‡Alan Howard Bede
Arthur Fillmore Altree	Albert Clarence Berg
Charles Jay Andersen	Nelson Conrad Block
‡Roger Elmer Anderson	Robert Ernest Boer
Maurice Joseph Aresty	†Robert Spence Bohrer
James Golvin Badger, Jr.	Douglas Ray Bolton
Herbert Herman Barnett	Joseph Borenstein
†Henry Bauling	Robert Eugene Bowman

‡*With Highest Distinction.*
†*With Distinction.*

Warren Edwin Bragg
Willis Charles Bremner
George William Brickwell
Robert Curtis Broberg
Albert Stanley Buividas
William Patrick Bulger
Myron Jack Butler
Raymond Phileas Chapleau
Franklin Jacob Charney
Lawrence Arnold Chez
Albert Russell Cobb, Jr.
Max Connelly
Mark Batchelder Conolly
Arthur Charles Daley
Robert Victor Damond
John Green Davidson
William Severight Davidson
Frederick Ernest Deatsman
Morton Deutsch
Norman Domash
William Francis Drohan, Jr.
George Reynolds Dutton
Bertil Paul Erikson
Ralph Ettlinger, Jr.
Carnot Wagener Evans
Ralph Arnold Feinstein
William Henry Fey
Ray Finkle, Jr.
Ralph Frederick Flora
Thomas Joseph Foley
Vernon Edward Force
Paul Henry Fortlage
Clesson Ward Freyer
Gordon Roger Frisbie
Lawrence Harry Frowick
David Frumkin
Lawrence Vernon Frye
Robert Watters Fulton
John Kenneth Funderburg
Thomas Yeates Gehr
Robert John Gerhardt
Samuel Gershuny
David Strangeway Gimbert
Lionel Miles Godow
David Daniel Golden
Allan Arnold Goldsmith
Robert James Gormley
John Joseph Grant
John Robert Green
Alfred Vernon Grove
Richard Leroy Haskell
Luther Albert Herbster
George Robert Hester
Harvey William Hielscher
Thomas Lawrence Hills

John Kipp Hoffrichter
Virginia Mae Hope
Stanley Hopper
Richard Clark Hoskins
Curtis Allen Huff
Ervin Adolph Husar, Jr.
Arnold Edgar Isaacson
Ralph Jay Isackson
Leslie James Johnson
Hugh Daniels Jones ʼ
Shirley Jane Kaye
James Alexander Kerr
Fred Fischer Klebe
Walter Emanual Klein
John Henry Kleine
Richard Jerome Kruger
Harold Louis Latin
Marshall Ronald Lavin
Robert DeBord Lawson
Ralph George Lee, Jr.
William Wallace Lee
Louis George Lenard
†Leon Lenkoff
‡John Philip Lindgren
Arnold Lester Lipkin
Richard Thomas Lochry
John Henry Luchow
Bertram Lutton
Robert James Lyon
William Madison
†Charles Russel Magel
Richard Burling Marquis
Robert Leon Mason
John William Masters
George Wesley Mattox
Mitchell Paul Mazurek
James Andrew McBride
Stuart Charles McKay
Axel Lynggaard Mikkelsen
Wilson Ervin Morgan
Gene Gordon Mundy
James Richard Murphy
James Wray Murray
Raymond Christ Nelsen
Verrazzano Simpson Nevius
Jay Newhof
Arthur Herbert Neyendorf, Jr.
Russell Charles Niccoli
‡Harold Isaac Niemi
Robert Francis Norton
‡Paul Reimer Nutt
Freidolph Kermit Olson
Henry Sundel Ovson
Charles Perry Paynter
†Leonard William Pedersen

‡*With Highest Distinction.*
†*With Distinction.*

[26]

Robert Edgar Pendarvis
James Sherman Penhallegon
Harold Francis Pfister, Jr.
Edward Theodore Podraza
Raymond Irving Post
Marguerite Agnes Postill
Edward Lee Renno
Jacob Estis Replogle, Jr.
Roy Reginald Roadcap
Ralph Howard Robertson
Jack Tuvin Rosen
†Sidney Ross
Frederick Acton Rowe, III
Bernard A. Rubin
†Raymond Wesley Salstrom
William Everett Scanlon
‡Elmer Jessen Scheer
Richard John Schnakenberg
Ralph Wendell Schuhart
Alvin Willis Schuman
Lois Harriet Schuman
Thomas Edward Sellinger
Robert Albert Sibrava
‡Harry D. Simon
LeRoy Alexander Smith

Leslie William Snudden
Kenneth Morris Sorensen
Allen Gilbert Spencer
John Edward Spiess
John Kenneth Spiller
Glenn Warren Stangeland
Wallace Raymond Stanz
James Gearld Stephenson
Morton David Stubins
Howard William Van Dis
Arthur Robert Van Tuinen
John Battista Vottero
Raymond Charles Wagner
Herbert Lawrence Wallerstein, Jr.
Claude Arnold Welles, Jr.
Herbert Joseph Wells
Robert Blair Wilkerson
Norman Edward Williams
Charles Armand Willis, Jr.
William Carl Willumsen, Jr.
Charles Harris Wilson, Jr.
William Henry Wolfe, Jr.
Claribel Emma Woods
Benjamin Martin Yanowitz

Diploma in Commerce

Alexander Hay Anderson
Burton Homer Atwood
William Edward Beck
Marvin Joseph Berger
Eberhard Siegfried Blanck
Gilbert Lowell Brooks
Gerald W. Bush
Frederick Emerson Byrd
Daniel Leo Campbell
Mark Carnahan
Anthony John Chromy
Ross Leroy Cochran
Catherine Cook
Richard Crisp
Robert David Fisher
Mariano Q. Galban
David Givertz
Eugene Goldberg
James Harkess
David Harris
Raymond Leonard Higgins
Carl Reese Johnson
Alfred Louis Kartsman
Leonard Onufry Kay
Clarence A. Keasling
Earl G. Koehler
Leonard Kolkey
Harry Kosovske

Martin Edward Lenihan
Walter Seitz Letzsch
Sanford Lieber
James Samuel Lillywhite
Robert Warren McClintock
Helen Frances McGillicuddy
Albert Howard Methe
Howard Clark Milliren
Estel Oliver Munson
Earl Andrew Myers
John Charles Newman
Seymour Oseas
†Carl Einar Pearson
George Edward Podlesak
Peter Przybylowicz
Carroll Edmund Quinn
Virgil Clendenning Rankin
John Edward Reed
Theodore Donald Roman
Lawrence Frank Rutstrom
Vladimir L. Rychly
Clifford Everett Sanders
Norman Bernard Schultz
George William Schwartz
Robert Loren Shanley
John Lee Smith
Norman John Smith
Richard Fred Stahlman

‡*With Highest Distinction.*
†*With Distinction.*

Adolph Edward Sterling
Harold David Strauss
Lloyd Hatch Strausz
George David Tolpo
Albert Sidney Tompkins
James F. Vodak, Jr.

Edwin Stewart Wheeler
Vernon Frank Wille
Roy R. Wixom
Rudolph Stanislaus Zapka
Chester George Zimmerman

BACHELOR OF SCIENCE IN SPEECH

Mildred Colette Barber
†Constance Parker Bard
Pauline Helen Barofsky
†Georgia Shewmake Bayless
Helen Elizabeth Bock
Betty Ann Brang
Eleanor Jane Burgett
William Henry Canfield
Charles James Carshon
Sheila Yvonne Clarke
Nora Pauline Culver
Eileen Marie Davis
Josephine Evelyn Dyer
George Ebenhack
Shirley Christine Ebner
Lyn Edwards
Betty Claire Ellis
Zelia Fidanque
Rosalyn Adele Freund
Helen Jane Friedman
Louis Georgius Geannopoulos
Cornelia Sill Green
†Kathryn Leighton Hall
Jean Lois Hartzell
Margaret Jane Haun
Elaine Thelma Hoenig
Catherine Irene Hopfinger
Richard Earl Jager
Kenneth Karl Jones, Jr.
Joyce Elaine Kennett
Verne Joseph Klaus
Mary Ethelyn de La Fontaine
    Knight
James William Knoernschild

Raymond Casimir Kostulski
Jean Elinor Krausé
†Richard Alan Langhinrichs
Sara Gadsden Lee
Audrey Leibowitz
Alberta Marie Lischesky
Jane Love
Peggy Loretta Lyons
Dorothy Lytle
Caroline Ann Magalhaes
Ruth Eleanor Marsh
Ruthmary McDowell
Edward Robertson McHale
Marjorie Minsk
Elizabeth Jane Norris
Julia Duncan Pagan
Marjorie Pickrell
Emily Hitch Pribble
Tova Quist
William Stuart Rent
Jeanne Betty Rothenberg
Ann Mavis St. John
Whitt Northmore Schultz
Geraldine Meek Semke
Helen Elizabeth Stevenson
Jeanne Louise Swanger
Gloria Beverly Taylor
Aljean Thurman Thomas
Wilmer Ernest Vess
Otis Monroe Walter, Jr.
Violet Pearl Wertens
Gloria Elma Wieber
Rita June Williams

MASTER OF SCIENCE IN EDUCATION

Olin Wilford Ellwood

Harry Lee Whitby

BACHELOR OF SCIENCE IN EDUCATION

Esther Abrams
*Adela Adamec
*Hazel Adamson
*Ethel Borghilde Andersen
Mary Ann Anderson
Mauree Applegate
*Reinhold Arkebauer
Ashley Eugene Arnold

Marjorie Constance Arnold
Paula Martha Assenheimer
Richard Atherton
Debra Eve Bambaloff
Margaret Amelia Barbery
Elizabeth Barnes
Alyce Ruth Bates
*Esther Browne Beasley

*Work completed through the University College.
†With Distinction.

*Ross Orville Beatty
Earl Louis Bell
George Paul Benson
*Ethel Berger
Frances Berline
Evelyn Gladys Berman
Betty Jane Bippus
‡Evelyn Lo Blue
Ernest Charles Bonhivert
*Paul Deckard Boyd
Esther Josephine Bratzler
Helen Braude
*Florence Caryl Breyer
*Katherine Briggs
†Dorothy Ruth Bronson
Elmire Isabelle Brown
*Louise Phillips Brown
*Rose Neeb Browne
*Viola Warren Burke
Eileen Mary Butler
*Alice Byrne
Anne Lara Caldwell
Alice Gladys Callan
Victor Camsky
Floyd Albert Chambers
Mary Ruth Chandler
Helen Gertrude Chubinski
Betty Blair Clarkson
Henry Edward Clason
Charles Donald Clawson
Craig Duane Clemons
Miriam Cohen
Joseph John Cook
*Laura Longstreet Cooper
*Elsie Cecile Couleur
*Julienne Louise Couleur
Bernice Delight Diamond
*Roberta Huff Dixon
Jean Doyle
Lynn Howard Draper
*Bettye Krawitz Ehrlich
*Dorothy Mildred Ehrlicher
*Ruth Mildred Erickson
*Rae Evans
Renee Harvey Fancher
Eva Lucille Fink
Caroline May Finkel
*Dorothye Frankel
*Mary Jeanette French
Evelyn Godfrey Ganns
Beatrice Ganzoff
*Virginia Gass
Harriette Jane Gifford
Robert Clarence Goeke
*Ruth Goldberg
Rachel Lucile Goldstein
Yvonne Grammer

Ida Gundersen
*Evaline Anna Hack
Barbara Jean Hamilton
Richard James Hanson
Ellen Julia Hardy
*Ella Harstad
Merrill Andrew Heagy
Donald Alvin Heintz
Barbara Ruth Heller
Howard Al Heller
Charles Stevens Hempelman
Beth Hindley
Elaine Phylis Hirschfield
Arlene Hazel Hoier
Beth Bertha Holthouse
Mary Elizabeth Hooton
Helen May Houghton
*Marion Agnes Hoyne
Arlene Elizabeth Huff
Mary Ann Humel
Beverly Hunt IlgenFritz
Phyllis Emelia Jacoby
Thomas Martin James
*John Hudson Jeffries
*Ruth Helen Jewell
Donald Clifford Johnson
Helen Florence Johnson
Elizabeth Jeannette Jones
Gloria Kathryn Jones
Shirley Ann Julien
Josephine Frances Kelly
Paul Frederick Kiefer
Jean Eleanor Killen
Marion Beverly Kirk
Wilma Marie Knoop
Violet Evelyn Kolar
Warren Herbert Kulieke
Jean Marilyn Lane
*La Verne Annette Larson
Ina Catharine Latta
Elizabeth Jane Leggitt
Sylvia Shirlee Lidsker
Adeline Lieberman
Gladys Gertrude Lifton
Edith Louise Lippincott
Peggy Littler
*Roy George Lundahl
Gladys Elaine Lundgren
*Martha Babette Maschmeyer
Evelyn Marie Mayer
Gladys Catherine Mazanec
Cathryn Ann McGinn
Lucille Freddye McKay
Gertrude McKeon
Eric McKinnon
Einar Knute Mehl

*Work completed through the University College.
‡With Highest Distinction.
†With Distinction.

Melverna Elaine Melville
Steven Meschuk
Jeanne Elizabeth Miller
*Wilbur Peter Miller
*Frank Miret
Irene Monahan
Ora Green Morrow
Mary Ruth Morse
Celia Mount
*Mildred Lucille Mueller
Mildred Jeannette Murphy
Elaine Marie Niehaus
Ruth Edna Neuffer
*Elizabeth Grace Noble
*Helen Eleanor Noble
Jeanne Marie Novy
Kathryn Eleanor O'Brien
Mavis Ordman
Mary Jane Orr
Gwendolyn Gair Osgood
*William Larkin Parker
Conrad Parkman
*Carmela Mildred Petrone
Ruth Evelyn Peterson
*Jean Florence Pitsner
Marial Charlotte Pliss
*Florence Porwancher
*Erma Provan
*Jennie Gladys Rankin
*Milton Raymer
*Marcella Barbour Reynolds
Arthur Henry Rissman
Edward Kenneth Roberts
Marvin Pershing Riley
Polly Battle Robinson
*Norma Fieldman Rogin
*Margaret Rohwer
Helen Mary Rolnick
*Mabel Lee Rowell
Elsa Doris Royack
*Lorraine Florence Rubin
Elizabeth La Verne Ruby
Jeanne Sacks
Marvin Nathaniel Samuel
*Evelyn Schiesser
Marvin Rolfe Scofield
*Anne Mourek Sebesta

Arthur Carl Serfling
*Gertrude Shapiro
*William Sheehan
*Anne Sherman
Mabel Siverson
Sanford Burton Skor
*Helen Skubikowski
Elinor Bird Sorensen
Helen Fay. Souders
Betty Jane Stober
Shirley Stockwell
*Lucile Anne Sullivan
Clara Helen Sunby
*Phyllis Surdyk
Irene Swenson
Helen Carpenter Taft
Dorothy Barbara Toman
Melvin Traylor
Mary Jane Tripple
*Gladys Vance
Lillian Margaret Vaughn
Duncan Frederic Vanderlip
Eileen Wallace
*Evelyn Agnes Waller
Betty Walters
Evelyn Warshauer
Myra Watson
*Mae Louisa Spiesman Werch
Marjorie Jane Welty
*Esther May Wetzel
*Gertrude Adler Whalley
Helen Elizabeth Wheaton
George Bridgeforth White
Mary Anne Whitley
Mary Elizabeth Wiegand
*Virginia Kent Williams
*Irene Hill Windstrup
*Goldie Winowsky
*Savilla Alleen Wise
Norman Anton Wodder
Janis Wolfson
Jean Louise Woodford
*Rosetta Phillips Wright
Alyce Louise Wykoff
*Eleanor Ann Young
*Milada Zrna

MASTER OF SCIENCE IN JOURNALISM

William Dean Bowden, B.A., Michigan State College, 1940.
George Custer Branston, B.S., Northwestern University, 1941.
Isabel Katherine Cumming, B.A., Wellesley College, 1940.
Joe Baird Egelhof, B.A., Loras College, 1940.
Lawrence Fein, B.S., Northwestern University, 1941.
Martha Louise Fidler, B.S., Northwestern University, 1942.

*Work completed through the University College.

†Carol Lynn Gilmer B.S., Honors Degree, Northwestern University, 1941.
†Robert Delmege Goodwin, B.S., Honors Degree, Northwestern University, 1941.
‡Dora Jane Hamblin, B.A., Coe College, 1941.
John Arberry Haney, B.S. in Speech, Northwestern University, 1940.
Russell Trovillo Hitt, A.B., University of Michigan, 1926.
Hoyt Hurst, A.B., Indiana State Teachers College, 1935.
Walter Beresford Lovelace, B.A., University of Colorado, 1940.
Louise Mary Lux.
Virginia Alice Mazurk, B.S., Northwestern University, 1941.
Mary Frances Payne, B.A., Illinois Wesleyan University, 1941.
Marshall Harold Peterson, B.S., Northwestern University, 1941.
Joan Goodman Rosenberg, B.A., University of Chicago, 1938.
William Henry Scrivner, B.S. in Commerce, Northwestern University, 1941.
†Raymond Carson Shady, B.S. in Commerce, Northwestern University, 1941.
Seymour Shlaes, B.S., Northwestern University, 1941.
Thein Tin, B.A., University of Rangoon, 1939.
†Carlin Alexander Treat, B.S., University of Santa Clara, 1940.
George Michael Watson, B.S., Northwestern University, 1941.

BACHELOR OF SCIENCE IN JOURNALISM

Glenn Wright McCoy

BACHELOR OF PHILOSOPHY

Embert Herman Almcrantz
Marjorie Tyler Buehler
Gilbert Sefton Faust
Raymond Lee Kahn
Julia Libuse Krbec
Earl Edwin Langdon

Frances Ailene Marks
Edwin Shouse Risk
Helen Rusch
Rebecca Levin Schoenfeld
Bernard Wajnberg
Eleanor Katherine Williams

DIPLOMA AS GRADUATE NURSE

Mary Elizabeth Arns
Jane Austin
Helen Marie Besola
Doris Marjorie Black
Helen Marie Eberhart
Gladys Elizabeth Eggert
Elizabeth Faye Fitszimmons
Elizabeth Marie Foels
Marian Elizabeth Forburger
Ruth Elizabeth Frish
Edythe Frances Gross
Hilda Bessie Hanson
Elisabeth Christine Hauch
Jane Heckenhauer
Patricia Jean Hubbell
Norma Helen Hubrig
Dorothy Jane Irving
Ruth Eleanore Jaehne
Harriet R. Loomis
Ursula Christa G. Mocksch
Patricia Estelle Moore
Felicitas Mary Moser
Constance Ella Nissen

Margaret Edna Olson
Margaret Louise Olson
Bonnie Maxine Orr
Helen Elizabeth Pedersen
Irene Lucille Petersen
Helen Elizabeth Rasmussen
Jean Lou Recktenwall
Helen Elfreda Rohwedder
Martha Elizabeth Schwieger
Mae Alper Simms
Betty Marion Simon
Elisabeth Skaropitsch
Lois LaVerne Spanabel
Crystal Marie Stoffel
Rangfred Sviland
Dorothy Ann Thomas
Mary Alice Thomson
Barbara Jean VanKirk
Caryl Eileen Walkington
Margaret Jane Williams
Helen Wojciechowska
Katherine Elise Yates

‡*With Highest Distinction.*
†*With Distinction.*

CERTIFICATE IN TRAFFIC ADMINISTRATION

George Wilbur Ashley
Joseph Gerald Baglin
James Joseph Basta
Ellsworth Robert Butz
Roy Frederick Carlson
Forrest Hiram Currens
George Daniel Eastman
Hudson Russell Hamm
Lloyd Wallace Henkel

James Donald Hill
Roland Humble
Fred Henry Miller
John Francis O'Neill
Robert Justin Routt
Conrad Bult Van Alen
Floyd Sydney Wakefield
Ambrose Penn Winston, Jr.

UNITED STATES NAVY
RESERVE COMMISSIONS

Roger Elmer Anderson
Mansfield Homer Beatty, Jr.
Alan Howard Bede
Robert Edward Bedessem
Robert Spence Bohrer
Willis Charles Bremner
Eugene Price Brown, Jr.
Merle Stephen Burdick
Floyd Albert Chambers
Craig Duane Clemons
Max R. Connelly
Bertil Paul Erikson
Robert Stuart French
John Kenneth Funderburg
Robert John Gerhardt
David Daniel Golden
Robert James Gormley
Frank Haldane Haigler, Jr.
John Kipp Hoffrichter
Joseph Albert Hollander, Jr.
Richard Clark Hoskins
Carl Arthur Hotze
Curtis Allen Huff
Paul Edward Hursh
Ervin Adolph Husar, Jr.

Robert William Kittredge
Leon G. Lenkoff
Richard Allen Lenon
Richard Thomas Lochry
William Roberts Love
Charles Russel Magel
Gregory Theodore McLean
Gene Gordon Mundy
Harold Isaac Niemi
Huston E. Olds
Leonard William Pedersen
Victor Samuel Peters
Lon Willing Ramsey
Roland Roderick Reiche
William Stuart Rent
Jacob Estis Replogle, Jr.
William Henry Scrivner
Raymond Carson Shady
John Thompson
Richard Arnold Trubey
Ralph Van Petten
Arthur Phillip Wandtke, Jr.
James Robertson Ward
Douglas Philip White
Layman John Wilkinson

DEGREES GRANTED DURING 1941-42

DOCTOR OF PHILOSOPHY
With Titles of Dissertations

Harry Frank Adler, S.B., University of Chicago, 1937; S.M., 1938. Physiology and Pharmacology. *Effects of Drugs on the Colon.*

William Campton Bell, B.S., Colorado Agricultural College, 1927; M.A., Northwestern University, 1935. Speech. *A History of the Denver Theater During the Post-Pioneer Period (1881-1901).*

James Philip Brawley, B.A., Samuel Huston College, 1920; M.A., Northwestern University, 1925. Education. *A Comparative Analysis of Certain Factors in the Dual Public School System of Georgia with Specific Reference to Financial Support, 1918-1938.*

[32]

Horace Brightberry Brown, Jr., B.S.C., University of Mississippi, 1931; M.B.A., Northwestern University, 1932. Marketing. *The Development and Present Status of the Cooperative Marketing of Cotton in the State of Mississippi.*

William Francis Brown, Jr., B.A., University of California at Los Angeles, 1933; M.A., 1934. Marketing. *Department Store Market Analysis.*

Pearl Bryant, B.A., Missouri Wesleyan College, 1921; M.A., Northwestern University, 1924. Speech. *Speech Re-education in the Nineteenth Century.*

Gladys Rosalin Bucher, B.S., Huron College, 1930; M.S., New York University, 1933. Physiology and Pharmacology. *Does Histamine Stimulate Pepsin Secretion?*

Harold Anderson Graver, B.A., Northwestern University, 1928; M.A., 1935. Education. *A Study of Student Personnel Needs at Northwestern University Dental School.*

Roderic Alfred Gregory, B.S., University of London, 1934; M.S., 1939. Physiology and Pharmacology. *The Humoral Mechanisms of Gastric Secretion.*

Erwin Taylor Katzoff, B.S., Northwestern University, 1935; M.A., 1939. Psychology. *Statistical Analyses of Individual Differences in Reaction to Experimental Situations.*

Freda Samuels Kramer, A.B., University of Illinois, 1916; A.M., University of South Dakota, 1935. Sociology. *The Program for Aid to Dependent Children in Minnesota, with Special Reference to its Administration and to the Adequacy of its Standards.*

Miriam Simons Leuck, Ph.B., University of Chicago, 1921; M.A., Northwestern University, 1923. History. *The American Socialist and Labor Mission to Europe, 1918; Background, Activities and Significance: An Experiment in Democratic Diplomacy.*

Robert Winston Liggett, B.S., University of Alberta, 1938. Chemistry. *The Separation and Identification of Carbohydrates.*

George Doss Lovell, A.B., Baylor University, 1938; M.A., Northwestern University, 1939. Psychology. *Physiological and Motor Responses to a Regularly Recurring Sound: A Study in Monotony.*

Martin Joseph Maloney, Jr., B.A., University of Kansas, 1937; M.A., 1938. Speech. *The Forensic Speaking of Clarence Darrow.*

John Martin, B.S., Lewis Institute, 1932; M.S., Northwestern University, 1934; M.D., 1935. Surgery. *Experimental and Clinical Observations Concerning the Results of Destruction of the Pineal Gland.*

Lee Mitchell, B.A. in Drama, Carnegie Institute of Technology, 1929; M.A. Northwestern University, 1936. Speech. *Elizabethan Scenes of Violence and the Problem of Their Staging.*

Ivan C. Nicholas, B.E., Northern Illinois State Teachers College, 1929; M.S. in Education, Northwestern University, 1934. Education. *The Status of the Working Relationship Between Boards of Education and City-School Superintendents in the State of Illinois.*

Richard Martin Page, B.A., University of Michigan, 1921; S.M., University of Chicago, 1932. Psychology. *Aggression and Withdrawal in Relation to Possible Frustrating Factors in the Lives of Children.*

Alonzo Smith Pond, A.B., University of Utah, 1926. Economics. *Urban Special Assessments in Down State Illinois, 1925-1937.*

Barbara Roth, B.S., Beloit College, 1937; M.S., Northwestern University, 1939. Chemistry. *Condensation Reaction of Olefinic Halides.*

Joseph Charles Seibert, B.S. in Business, Miami University, 1932; M.B.A., Northwestern University, 1933. Marketing. *Price Behavior and Industrial Activity.*

Anna Markt Shotwell, B.A., Northwestern University, 1925; M.A., 1928. Psychology. *Five- and Ten-Year-Old Children's Concepts of Mother.*

James Spencer Strong, B.A., Ohio State University, 1937. Chemistry. *Reactions of the Nitroparaffins.*

James Donald Watson, B.A., Reed College, 1926; M.B.A., University of Michigan, 1931. Political Science. *Public Accounting System in Indiana.*

Ruth Fox Wyatt, Ph.B., University of Chicago, 1927; B.M.E., Northwestern University, 1931; M.A., 1935. Psychology. *The Improvability of Pitch Discrimination.*

MASTER OF ARTS

Ella Marie Abbott, B.S. in Education, Northwestern University, 1930. Education.
Isadore Abraham, B.S. in Chemical Engineering, Armour Institute of Technology, 1931. Education.
James Truax Achuff, B.S., Milwaukee State Teachers College, 1938. Education.
Jessie Mae Agnew, A.B., Colorado State College of Education, 1938. Education.
Mary Margaret Alcorn, A.B., Eureka College, 1930. Education.
Anna Mary Allen, B.A., Central Y.M.C.A. College, 1940. Social Work.
John Stevens Allen, B.A., Williams College, 1938. English.
Dorothy Margaret Allison, A.B., Hanover College, 1940. Speech.
Dorothy Edison Alter, B.S., Lewis Institute, 1937. Social Work.
Lewis William Amborn, B.S., University of Wisconsin, 1927. Education.
Dorothea Ammerman, B.S., Northwestern University, 1940. Education.
Melvin Adolph Anderson, B.Ed., Northern Illinois State Teachers College, 1936. Education.
Whitney Edward Anderson, B.S. in Education, Northwestern University, 1939. Education.
Stuart Harris Andrews, B.Ed., State Teachers College, Whitewater, Wisconsin, 1938. Education.
Anne Belle Anslow, B.Ed., National College of Education, 1937. Education.
Doris Elizabeth Armstrong, B.S., University of Oklahoma, 1938. Education.
Josephine Hahn Arthur, B.S., Northwestern University, 1928. Social Work.
Frank Howard Ashcraft, B.Ed., State Teachers College, Whitewater, Wisconsin, 1930. Education.
Robert Jordan Atkins, B.S.A.S., Lewis Institute, 1937. History.
John George Ausman, B.S., Stout Institute, 1934. Education.
Arthur James Aylward, B.Ed., State Teachers College, Whitewater, Wisconsin, 1937. Education.
Ernest L. Badenoch, B.S. in Speech, Northwestern University, 1940. Speech.
Mardelle Lucille Bahr, B.S. in Education, Northwestern University, 1940. Education.
Harriet Grace Baird, B.A., University of Wisconsin, 1925. Education.
Jeanette Irwin Baird, B.A., Monmouth College, 1935. Education.
Mary Elizabeth Baird, B.A., University of Wisconsin, 1923. Education.
Arthur Basse, B.A., Amherst College, 1940. Economics.
Ellery Frost Bassler, B.Ed., Central State Teachers College, Wisconsin, 1937. Education.
Stephen Selig Baumann, B.S., George Williams College, 1937. Social Work.
Ellen Agnes Baxter, B.S., University of Minnesota, 1930. Education.
Marion Eleanor Beatty, A.B., Smith College, 1939. English.
John Hamilton Beck, B.S. in Speech, Northwestern University, 1932. Speech.
Jane Gans Becker, B.A., Northwestern University, 1939. Classical Languages.
Charles Monroe Behrman, B.S. in Education, Ball State Teachers College, 1939. Education.
Edith Benjamin, Ph.B., University of Chicago, 1928. Education.
Kathryn Elizabeth Bennett, A.B., University of California, 1927. Education.
Elizabeth Alice Benson, B.S. in Education, Northwestern University, 1935. Education.
Stanley Carroll Benz, B.A., Iowa State Teachers College, 1937. Education.
Jacob Bercovitz, B.S., Northwestern University, 1931. Social Work.
Robert John Bickel, B.A., University of Louisville, 1937. Mathematics.
Barbara Bixby, B.Ed., Milwaukee State Teachers College, 1934. Education.
Helen Blakely, B.Ed., Northern Illinois State Teachers College, 1938. Education.
Gerald Lynn Bodine, B.S. in Ed., State Teachers College, Whitewater, Wisconsin, 1937. Education.
Helen Hayes Bone, B.S., Purdue University, 1928. Speech.
Bonnie Beatrice Bonthron, B.A., Lawrence College, 1938. Education.
Edith Rosenbloom Borison, B.S. in Education, University of Illinois, 1932. Social Work.
Bruce Otis Bower, B.S. in Education, Ohio University, 1937. Education.

Merton Russell Bowyer, B.Ed., State Teacher's College, Whitewater, Wisconsin, 1938. Education.

Georgia Mae Brader, B.S., Oklahoma College for Women, 1925. Social Work.

Florence Brandenburger, B.Ed., National College of Education, 1937. Education.

Daniel Charles Brandner, B.S. in Education, Kansas State Teachers College of Emporia, 1933. Political Science.

Susan Virginia Brandon, B.S. in Education, Teachers College of Kansas City, 1940. Education.

Lester Raymond Breniman, B.A., Parsons College, 1927. Speech.

Alvin George Brooks, B.S., Northwestern University, 1938. Social Work.

Ada Elizabeth Brown, B.S. in Education, University of Illinois, 1937. Education.

Booker Phillips Brown, B.S., Colored Agricultural and Normal University, 1933. Education.

Guy Harold Brown, B.S., State Teachers College, River Falls, Wisconsin, 1939. Education.

Kathryn Margaret Brown, B.A., Knox College, 1940. Education.

Ruby Elizabeth Brown, A.B., The Rice Institute, 1932. Education.

Sarah Elizabeth Brown, A.B., DePauw University, 1938. History.

Alma Lydia Bubeck, B.S., State Teachers College, Eau Claire, Wisconsin, 1938. Education.

Helena Anne Bubeck, B.Ed., State Teachers College, Eau Claire, Wisconsin, 1936. Education.

Anna Louise Buck, B.A., University of Michigan, 1926. Social Work.

Arthur Buehler, B.P.E., Normal College of American Gymnastic Union, 1935. Education.

Beverly Irene Burg, B.A., University of Wisconsin, 1936. Social Work.

Donald Thomas Burton, B.Ed., State Teachers College, Whitewater, Wisconsin, 1932. Education.

Mary Ella Bushong, B.S., Indiana Central College, 1926. Education.

Glen Gilbert Cady, B.S. in Business Administration, Simpson College, 1927. Education.

Mary Honor Callanan, Ph.B., Loyola University, 1931. Education.

Isabel Errington Callvert, B.A., Mills College, 1933. Speech.

Joe Ivan Cantrell, B.S. in Education, Southwest Missouri State Teachers College, 1930. Education.

Thelma Robuck Capp, B.A., B.E., Mary Hardin-Baylor College, 1935. Speech.

Clara Othelia Carlson, B.A., Augustana College, 1924. Education.

Gertrude Christine Carlson, B.A., Municipal University, 1932. Social Work.

Julia Webster Carroll, B.S. in Speech, Northwestern University, 1940. Speech.

William Scott Carter, B.S. in Education, Northwestern University, 1939. Education.

Jane Pine Casey, B.A., University of Wisconsin, 1919. Education.

Walter Frank Cebelin, B.B.A., Central Y.M.C.A. College, 1938. Education.

Catherine Singer Chessick, B.A. (equivalent), Prater Girl's College of Budapest, 1922. Social Work.

Myron Robert Chevlin, B.S., Northwestern University, 1939. Social Work.

Richard Henry Chowen, A.B., University of Illinois, 1939. History.

Alphus Rolland Christensen, B.S., South Dakota State College, 1938. Speech.

Frances Burns Christner, A.B., Western State Teachers College, 1937. Education.

Doris Rose Christopher, B.Ed., Pestalozzi-Froebel Teachers College, 1937. Education.

Eleanor Milward Clark, B.S. in Speech, Northwestern University, 1936. Speech.

Miriam Goddard Clark, B.A., Radcliffe College, 1936. Social Work.

Norman Robert Clayton, B.A., Carroll College, 1934. Education.

Joseph Cohen, B.S., Northwestern University, 1939. Sociology.

Kenneth Milburn Collier, B.S. in Education, Ball State Teachers College, 1938. Education.

Virginia Congreve, B.S. in Education, Northwestern University, 1939. Education.

Rhoda Malee Conrad, B.A., State University of Iowa, 1932. Education.

James Cook, B.S., North Central College, 1929. Education.

Allie Marie Coon, B.A., State Teachers College, Oshkosh, Wisconsin; 1938. Education.

Robert Orrin Cordts, B.Ed., State Teachers College, Platteville, Wisconsin, 1936. Education.
Myra May Corse, B.Ed., Western Illinois State Teachers College, 1933. Education.
James Carl Cotter, B,S., Northwestern University, 1935. Social Work.
Charles Reeffe Crakes, B.S. in Education, Northwestern University, 1930. Education.
Ralph Crow, B.Ed., Milwaukee State Teachers College, 1935. Education.
Dana Arlene Crowell, B.S. in Commerce, Northwestern University, 1926. Education.
Edith May Cumming, B.Ed., State Teachers College, Whitewater, Wisconsin, 1930. Education.
Earle Muller Curtiss, A.B., University of Illinois, 1923. Education.
Robert Lee Danzig, A.B., Indiana University, 1937. Social Work.
Lucy Davies, B.S. in Education, Northwestern University, 1939. English.
Elizabeth Woolfolk Davis, A.B., Transylvania College, 1938. Mathematics.
Orrel Davis, B.A., Northwestern University, 1927. Education.
Nellie Maud Day, Ph.B., University of Chicago, 1936. Education.
Robert Francis DeRoo, B.S. in Physical Education, North Central College, 1939. Education.
Margaret Edna DeWeese, B.A., State University of Iowa, 1935. Education.
Robert Charles Dickey, B.A., Monmouth College, 1933. Education.
Roy Richard Dillon, B.Ed., Illinois State Normal University, 1937. Education.
Anne Pauline Donoghue, B.A., Greenville College, 1923. Education.
Carlton Boice Doughty, B.S., Ohio Northern University, 1936. Education.
Jack Erskine Douglas, B.A., University of Oklahoma, 1936. Speech.
Dean E. Douglass, B.S., Central Missouri State Teachers College, 1926. Education.
Lucy Eleanor Doyle, B.A., University of Wisconsin, 1938. Education.
Lloyd A. Drexler, B.S., Northwestern University, 1939. Economics.
Imogene Dunton, B.S. in Industrial Education, State Normal and Industrial School, 1928. Education.
Ruth Weske Durlacher, B.S. in Education, Northwestern University, 1934. Education.
Dale Durnford, B.Ed., State Teachers College, La Crosse, Wisconsin, 1939. Education.
David E. DuVall, B.Ed., Minnesota State Teachers College, 1937. Education.
Muriel Jeanette Edwards, B.Ed., Eastern Illinois State Teachers College, 1935. Education.
Sam Herman England, B.S. in Education, Northwest Missouri State Teachers College, 1926. Education.
Emma Josephine Erickson, B.Ed., Winona Teachers College, 1928. Education.
Alfhild Helene Ericson, B.S. in Education, Northwestern University, 1931. English.
Ethel Louise Farthing, B.A., Bradley Polytechnic Institute, 1931. History.
Betty Lee Feldman, B.S. in Education, DePaul University, 1931. Education.
Ella Marie Fenwick, A.B., Western State Teachers College, 1940. Education.
William Bruce Ferry, B.Ed., Northern Illinois State Teachers College, 1935. Education.
Gershon Barnett Ferson, Ph.B., University of Chicago, 1933. English.
Walter Fredrick Fierke, B.S., Bradley Polytechnic Institute, 1932. Education.
Beatrice Theresa Flaherty, B.Ed., Milwaukee State Teachers College, 1936. Education.
Mildred Wessner Flaskered, B.S., Northwestern University, 1931. Education.
Ross Jean Fligor, B.Ed., Southern Illinois State Normal University, 1937. Education.
John Charles Foti, B.Ed., Milwaukee State Teachers College, 1932. Education.
Leslie Howard Fox, Jr., B.A., Temple University, 1934. Speech.
Ruth Muriel Freiss, B.F.A. in Education, University of Nebraska, 1937. Education.
Ruby Elsbeth Fremont, S.B., University of Chicago, 1921. Education.
Elsie Louise French, B.A., University of Utah, 1933. Education.
Esther Higgins Frey, Ph.B., University of Chicago. 1932. Education.
Helenmary Fritsch, A.B., Florida State College for Women, 1935. English.
Fannie Furman, B.A., University of Wisconsin, 1926. Social Work.
Mildred Futor, B.S. in Education, University of Oklahoma, 1935. Education.
Lucille Elizabeth Gaedke, B.Ed., State Teachers College, Whitewater, Wisconsin, 1935. Education.
Wofford Gordon Gardner, B.A., Southwestern College, 1935. Speech.

Bessie Eunice Garrison, B.A., University of Colorado, 1938. History.
Antone Alden Geisert, A.B., Indiana State Normal School, 1924. Education.
Albert E. Gibas, B.S., Northwestern University, 1938. Art.
Helen Genevieve Gibbons, B.A., Rosary College, 1933. Education.
Labelle Gillespie, A.B., Drury College, 1932. English.
Ruth Hunt Glaze, B.S., Texas State College for Women, 1938. Education.
Evelyn Gertrude Gleason, Ph.B., Loyola University, 1935. Education.
Ruth BellhGober, B.F.A. in Expression, University of Oklahoma, 1925; B.A., 1928. Speech.
Clifford Elger Goerke, B.A., Carroll College, 1931. Education.
Johanna Myra Goldberg, B.S. in Education, Northwestern University, 1934. Education.
Charles Goldstein, B.S., Lewis Institute, 1937. Social Work.
Andrew J. Goodman, B.Ed., State Teachers College, Whitewater, Wisconsin, 1939, Education.
Louis B. Goodrich, B.A., College of Emporia, Kansas, 1925. Education.
Betty Kirby Grady, B.S., Northwestern University, 1940. Education.
Gussie Grusin Green, S.B., University of Chicago, 1928. Education.
Herbert Julius Greenberg, B.S., Northwestern University, 1940. Mathematics.
Edna Joana Gregg, Ph.B., University of Chicago, 1924. Education.
Thais Martha Greulach, B.S. in Education, Butler University, 1939. Education.
Tella Griffin, Ph.B., University of Wisconsin, 1927. Education.
Ruth Elsie Gruel, B.Ed., Milwaukee State Teachers College, 1934. Education.
Otto Carl Haack, B.S., The Stout Institute, 1931. Education.
Evelyn Hallowell, B.Ed., Eastern Illinois State Teachers College, 1935. Education.
Lois Viola Hamer, B.A., Iowa State Teachers College, 1937. Education.
Louise Graham Hamilton, B.S. in Education, Northwestern University, 1926. Education.
Marion Palmer Hamilton, A.B., University of Illinois, 1924. Social Work.
Margarette Blanche Hammond, A.B., Western State Teachers College, 1939. Education.
Arthur W. Hancock, B.A., Wheaton College, 1921. Education.
Samuel Handler, B.S. in Education, State Teachers College at Buffalo, 1934. Social Work.
Geneva Regula Hanna, B.A., Hamline University, 1937. Education.
Paul Jennings Hannahs, A.B., University of Illinois, 1933. Education.
Gertrude Audrey Hargreaves, B.A., Cornell College, 1940. English.
Julius Norman Harris, Ph.B., University of Chicago, 1919. Education.
Marjorie Kipp Harris, B.S., Northwestern University, 1931. Social Work.
Dorothy Harrod, A.B., Knox College, 1925. Education.
Janet H. Harvey, B.A., Northwestern University, 1917. Education.
Kenneth W. Haubenschild, B.Ed., State Teachers College, Whitewater, Wisconsin, 1935. Education.
Sara A. Hawkinson, A.B., Midland College, 1934. Speech.
Mary Lois Heflebower, B.S. in Speech, Northwestern University, 1939. Speech.
Mae Hendrickson, A.B., Illinois Wesleyan University, 1938. Social Work.
Bernice Fern Henry, B.A., University of Illinois, 1923. English.
Norma Lurine Hess, B.S. in Education, Northwestern University, 1940. Education.
Romeyn Hess, A.B., Rockford College, 1938. Social Work.
Harold Eugene Hickman, A.B., DePauw University, 1936. Education.
Nina Climena Hill, B.S., Oklahoma A. & M. College, 1926. Education.
Selma Hill, A.B., University of Nebraska, 1940. Education.
Frank M. Himmelman, B.S., Milwaukee State Teachers College, 1938. Education.
Esther Alberta Hinds, B.A., University of Manitoba, 1926. Education.
Ruth Elizabeth Hines, B.S., Northwestern University, 1938. Social Work.
Eugene Quinter Hoak, A.B., Wittenberg College, 1937. Speech.
James Clinton Hodge, B.Ed., Illinois State Normal University, 1938. Education.
Earl Ellis Hoff, S.B., University of Chicago, 1924. Education.
Virginia Lydia Hollis, B.S. in Education, University of Louisville, 1935. Education.
Arthur Alvin Hoops, B.Ed., State Teachers College, Whitewater, Wisconsin, 1938. Education.
Shirley Colene Hoose, A.B., Illinois Wesleyan University, 1930. Speech.

[37]

Gladys Mary Horn, B.S., Teachers College, Columbia University, 1935. Education.
Gordon Douglass Howard, B.S. in Speech, Northwestern University, 1938. Speech.
Thelma Howey, B.S., University of the City of Toledo, 1928. Education.
Rosamond Huff, B.A., Carroll College, 1932. Education.
Elnora Maxine Humphrey, B.S., Colored Agricultural and Normal University, 1935.
    Education.
Clarence Alphonse Hunt, B.A., Dillard University, 1929. Education.
Mary Elizabeth Hyde, B.S., University of Illinois, 1931. Education.
Anna Laura Hyer, B.S., Purdue University, 1932. Education.
Harold Allen Hyer, B.S., Stout Institute, 1932. Education.
Rebecca Scofield Jackson, B.S. in Education, Northwestern. University, 1936.
    Education.
Grace Atkins Jason, B.S., Hampton Normal & Agricultural Institute, 1933. Education.
Anne Marion Jenkins, A.B., University of Denver, 1932. Education.
Alice Marie Jensen, B.S. in Education, Northwestern University, 1938. Education.
Raymond M. Jenson, B.S., Midland College, 1936. Education.
Francis Earl Joas, B.S., The Stout Institute, 1930. Education.
Avis Joan Johnson, B.S., Michigan State Normal College, 1930. Education.
Dorothy May Johnson, Ph.B., University of Chicago, 1934; B.F.A., Art Institute,
    1937. Art.
Elizabeth Marie Johnson, B.Ed., State Teachers College, Whitewater, Wisconsin,
    1929. Education.
Elyn Victoria Johnson, B.S., McKendree College, 1912. Education.
Romelle Helen Johnson, B.Ed., State Teachers College, Whitewater, Wisconsin, 1938.
    Education.
Annamae Marguerite Jones, B.S. in Education, Northeast Missouri State Teachers
    College, 1938. Education.
Margaret Jones, B.S. in Education, University of Washington, 1932. Speech.
David Leon Kaplan, B.S. in Speech, Northwestern University, 1940. Speech.
Antoinette Catherine Karabin, B.Ed., Pestalozzi-Froebel Teachers College, 1937.
    Education.
J. Grover Kelly, B.S., University of Utah, 1939. Speech.
Edith H. Kenrick, B.S. in Education, Northwestern University, 1938. Education.
Vernon Edward Keye, B.A., Beloit College, 1932. Social Work.
Dellema Jeannette King, B.S. in Education, Northwestern University, 1930. Education.
Mayme Edith King, A.B., McPherson College, 1922. Speech.
Elizabeth Kingsley, B.A., Wellesley College, 1933. Social Work.
Mabel Florence Kirk, B.A., Western Reserve University, 1925. Education.
Chester Arthur Kirkendoll, A.B., Lane College, 1938. Education.
Dorothy Hopkins Kirkland, B.L.T., Emerson College of Oratory, 1921. Speech.
Hugo Klann, B.Ed., State Teachers College, Whitewater, Wisconsin, 1939. Education.
Robert Louis Klausmeier, B.S. in Civil Engineering, Purdue University, 1933; B.D.,
    Garrett Biblical Institute, 1939. Education.
Evelyn L. Kletzing, B.A., Northwestern University, 1915. Speech.
Russell D. Knapp, B.Ed., Milwaukee State Teachers College, 1934. Education.
Barbara Jean Koenig, B.A., Northwestern University, 1939. Education.
Chester John Kowal, B.Ed., Western Illinois State Teachers College, 1939. Education.
Herbert Herman Kraneman, A.B., John B. Stetson University, 1936. Education.
Florence May Kriegsman, A.B., University of Illinois, 1924. Education.
Joseph Krob, B.S., Central Y.M.C.A. College, 1936. Education.
Agnes Elizabeth Krog, B.L., Northwestern University, 1924. Speech.
Nellie Naomi Langford, A.B., Colorado State College of Education, 1929. Education.
Dorothy Moore LaRue, A.B., B.S., University of Missouri, 1936. Education.
Kathleen Nace Laubach, B.A., Cedar Crest College, 1935. Speech.
Jack Milton Lear, B.A., Carleton College, 1939. Social Work.
Annabel Lee, B.S. in Education, Teachers College of Kansas City, 1935. Education.
Elsie Judith Lehtimaki, B.S., Northern State Teachers College, 1932. Education.
Ethel Levin, B.S., Texas State College for Women, 1936. Speech.
Margarette Bufe Liedberg, B.A., Monmouth College, 1933. Education.

Lucile Harriett Lindberg, B.S. in Education, Northwest Missouri State Teachers College, 1936. Education.
Mildred Valerie Linzer, B.S., Northwestern University, 1938. Social Work.
Walter Cecil Loague, B.A., Johns Hopkins University, 1917; B.D., Garrett Biblical Institute, 1920. Social Work.·
Cecile Mary Logic, B.Ed., State Teachers College, Whitewater, Wisconsin, 1938. Education. ·
Alfred H. Loken, Ph.B., University of Wisconsin, 1931. Education.
Milton Lomask, B.A., State University of Iowa, 1930. Speech.
Mary Elizabeth Loughborough, B.S. in Education, Northwestern University, 1938. Education.
Carolyn Sawyer Lowry, A.B.,·University of Illinois, 1937.. Social Work.
Helen Elizabeth Ludwig, B.A., Coe College, 1929. Education.·
Viona Helen Luhtala, Ph.B., University of Chicago, 1937. Education.
Richard Thompson Lumby, A.B., DePauw University, 1937. Education.
Richard Vernon Lybeck, A.B., Luther College, 1929. Education.
Mabel Lucy Lynn, B.S. in Education, University of Kansas, 1934. Education.
Ruth Magidson, A.B., Hunter College, 1936. Social Work.
William Anthony Mahoney, B.A., University of New Hampshire, 1929. Education.
John Edward Maier, B.Ed., Central State Teachers College, Wisconsin, 1937. Education.
Maurice Maloff, B.S.A.S., Lewis Institute, 1936. Education.
Gladys Ellen Manship, B.A., Northwestern University, 1923. English.
Rebecca Marcus, B.S., Northwestern University, 1936. Social Work.·
Mary A. Mark, B.S. in Education, Northwestern University, 1938. English.
Inez Elizabeth Martelle, B.Ed., State Teachers College, La Crosse, Wisconsin, 1934. Education.
Isabel Childs Martin, B.S. in Education, Drake University, 1928. Education.
Mary Ann Matthews, A.B., University of Chicago, 1939. Education.
Jeanette Victoria Mazur, B.S.A.S., Lewis Institute, 1934. Education.
Eugene Hugh McCusker, B.S., University of North Dakota, 1931. Education.
Helen Logan McDonnell, A.B., Dickinson College, 1928. Education.
Eleanor McFall, B.A., Grinnell College, 1932. Education.
Robert Mitchell McKenzie, B.D., Gammon Theological Seminary, 1911. Education.
Marguerite Lockhart McNall, Ph.B., University of Chicago, 1931. Education.
Wilda Mae Merritt, A.B., San Jose State Teachers College, 1938. Speech.
Mildred Esther Mettling, B.A., Southwestern College, 1939. Education.
Frederick William Meyers, B.A., Morningside College, 1937. Education.
Ellen Gertrude Miller, B.A., Iowa State Teachers College, 1937. Education.
Helen Jo Miller, B.S., Nebraska Wesleyan University, 1931. Education.
Katharine Mildred Minshall, B.S., Eastern State Teachers College, 1929. Education.
Jule Mishkin, B.S.L., Northwestern University, 1925; J.D., 1926. Education.
John Misun, B.S., Milwaukee State Teachers College, 1938. Education.
John Dietrich Mitchell, B.S. in Speech, Northwestern University, 1939.. Speech.
Rose Marie Mohrdieck, A.B., MacMurray College for Women, 1938. Speech.
Jerome William Mohrhusen, B.S., University of Wisconsin, 1935. Education.·
Charlotte A. Moody, B.A., State University of Iowa, 1918. Education.
Andrew Alexander Moore, B.S. in Education, Northwestern University, 1938. Education. ·
Madeline Robinson Morgan, B.S. in Education, Northwestern University, 1936. Education.
Grace Elaine Morris, B.S. in Speech, Northwestern University, 1936. Social Work.
Kyle Randolph Morris, B.A., Northwestern University, 1939. Art.
Ruth Emma Morris, B.A., Ripon College, 1928. Education.
Ruth Joanne Morris, B.S. in Journalism, University of Illinois, 1938. Social Work.
Frances Allyn Moss, B.S. in Education, Northwestern University, 1938. Education.
Nicholas Allison Moss, B.S., Davidson College, 1933. Speech.
Ann Katherine Mosser, B.A., Northwestern University, 1938. Education.
Genevieve Marie Mulcahy, B.M.E., American Conservatory of Music, 1939. Education.

Royal Stanley Myers, B.Ed., Southern Illinois State Teachers College, 1934. Education.
Halena Gould Nelson, B.Ed., Illinois State Normal University, 1933. Education.
Lawrence Milton Nelson, B.Ed., Illinois State Normal University, 1937. Education.
Leonore Reque Newell, B.A., St. Olaf College, 1927. Education.
Elmer T. Nicholas, B.Ed., State Teachers College, La Crosse, Wisconsin, 1928. Education.
Bernys Surkin Nierman, Ph.B., University of Chicago, 1934. Social Work.
Helen Bernice Nimtz, B.Ed., Central State Teachers College, Wisconsin, 1936. Education.
Evelyn Mildred Nolan, B.S. in Education, DePaul University, 1932. Education.
Helen Ursula Novack, B.S., University of Wisconsin, 1933. Education.
Florence Ann O'Callahan, A.B., Mundelein College, 1937. Education.
Dorothy Powell Oldendorf, B.S. in Education, Northwestern University, 1939. Education.
Anne Westrom Olson, B.S., Iowa State College of Agriculture and Mechanic Arts, 1926. Psychology.
George Andrew Olson, B.S., Wheaton College, 1934. Education.
Clarence F. Omacht, B.Ed., State Teachers College, St. Cloud, Minnesota, 1937. Education.
Daniel John O'Neill, B.S. in Education, DePaul University, 1933. Education.
Loretta Myrtle Ortt, B.S., Western State Teachers College, 1937. Education.
Helen May Osberg, B.S. in Education, Northwestern University, 1938. Education.
Mary B. Ostlund, A.B., Brigham Young University, 1928. Education.
Albertine Mildred Palmer, B.S. in Education, Northwestern University, 1935. Education.
W. Russell Palmer, B.A., Grinnell College, 1924. Education.
Nicholas Joseph Panella, B.A., Carroll College, 1923. Education.
Doris Campbell Patrick, B.A., State University of Iowa, 1932. Speech.
Jean Juanita Patrick, B.S., Northwest Missouri State Teachers College, 1935. Education.
Agnes Jane Patton, B.S. in Education, Northwestern University, 1939. Education.
Frances Eleanor Peacock, A.B., Indiana University, 1927. English.
Florence Isabel Peeken, B.Ed., Illinois State Normal University, 1938. Education.
Miriam Horwitz Peizer, B.S. in Education, Northwestern University, 1931. Social Work.
Audra May Pence, B.S. in Education, Northeast Missouri State Teachers College, 1935. Education.
Harvey Perlman, B.A., Central Y.M.C.A. College, 1939. Social Work.
Hilding Gunnar Peterson, B.A., Macalester College, 1937. Speech.
Lorraine Marion Peterson, B.Ed., State Teachers College, Eau Claire, Wisconsin, 1937. Education.
George Thomas Phelan, B.A., Loras College, 1937. Education.
Susanne Claire Pick, B.A., Rollins College, 1939. Education.
Claire Anne Plantinga, A.B., Calvin College, 1940. Education.
Julius Alberding Plapp, B.Ed., Northern Illinois State Teachers College, 1935. Education.
Lyle Clifford Pollock, B.Ed., State Teachers College, Whitewater, Wisconsin, 1931. Education.
Charles Wesley Poppenheimer, B.A., Iowa State Teachers College, 1938. Education.
Morgan A. Poullette, B.Ed., State Teachers College, Oshkosh, Wisconsin, 1935. Education.
Mary Ella Powell, B.Ed., Southern Illinois State Normal University, 1934. Education.
Mary Elizabeth Powell, B.S. in Education, University of Missouri, 1935. Education.
Mayola Margarite Powers, A.B. in Education, University of Michigan, 1932. Education.
Violet Keats Prugger, B.A., Northwestern University, 1919. Education.
Goldie Marie Pugh, A.B., Western College, 1917. Social Work.
Kathryn Helen Quinlan, Ph.B., University of Chicago, 1937. Education.
Margaret Radcliffe, B.A., B.S. in Education, University of North Dakota, 1927. English.

Ralph Kenneth Rader, B.Ed., Illinois State Normal University, 1936. Education.
Charles William Rainey, A.B., Indiana University, 1938. Speech.
Philip Westbrook Ramer, B.Ed., Northern Illinois State Teachers College, 1931. Education.
Isabelle Cecilia Ramstad, B.A., Concordia College, 1923. Education.
Robert S. Ratcliffe, A.B., Indiana State Teachers College, 1940. Speech.
Francis Patrick Ready, B.A., DePaul University, 1939. Latin.
Ruth Winifred Redwine, B.A., Oklahoma University, 1926. Speech.
Janet Catherine Rees, B.Ed., National College of Education, 1933. Education.
Ethel Lucille Rice, B.Ed., State Teachers College, Whitewater, Wisconsin, 1932. Education.
James Andrew Rickhoff, B.S., Lewis Institute, 1936. Education.
Ruth Jeannette Ringland, A.B., Cornell College, 1930. Speech.
Robert Douglas Rippeta, A.B., University of Missouri, 1937. Social Work.
Ada Elizabeth Ritz, B.A., Northwestern University, 1939. Education.
Blanche Berson Robbins, Ph.B., University of Chicago, 1933. Education.
Mary Jane Roberts, B.S. in Home Economics, Montana State College, 1934. Education.
Raymond Arland Roberts, B.S. in Education, Northwest Missouri State Teachers College, 1936. Education.
Ora Aileen Rodeniser, A.B., Dakota Wesleyan University, 1932. Speech.
Gladys May Rohrig, A.B., DePauw University, 1930. Speech.
Harrison Oather Rose, A.B., Muskingum College, 1932. Speech.
Audre Mae Ross, B.Ed., Southern Illinois State Normal University, 1932. Education.
Jack Charles Rossetter, B.Ed., Illinois State Normal University, 1934. Education.
Helen Irene Rossiter, B.Ed., Eastern Illinois State Teachers College, 1933. Education.
Helen Catherine Roth, A.B., Western College, 1929. Education.
Helen L. Rothgeb, B.Ed., Western Illinois State Teachers College, 1934. Education.
Elizabeth Routt, A.B., Georgetown College, 1928. Education.
Ida Byrd Rowe, A.B., Anderson College and Theological Seminary, 1936. Education.
Charles James Ruddy, A.B., DePaul University, 1928. Education.
Ethel Mae Rumpf, B.Ed., State Teachers College, La Crosse, Wisconsin, 1934. Education.
Albert F. Ryan, B.Ed., Southern Illinois State Normal University, 1933. Education.
Loretto Aloyse Ryan, Ph.B., University of Chicago, 1932. English.
Arthur Hilding Ryden, B.A., DePauw University, 1940. Education.
Alfred Gerhurd Ryll, B.S., Western State Teachers College, 1939. Education.
Evelyn Marie Saduske, B.Ed., State Teachers College, Whitewater, Wisconsin, 1938. Education.
Ethel Blanche Sager, B.A., College of Wooster, 1921. Latin.
Kathryn Hurley Sands, Ph.B., Loyola University, 1927. Education.
Orville James Sayers, B.Ed., Illinois State Normal University, 1936. Education.
Margaret Mary Scannell, B.Ed., Milwaukee State Teachers College, 1933. Education.
Valentine Walter Schaller, B.S., Milwaukee State Teachers College, 1938. Education.
Arnold Carl Scheer, B.S., Milwaukee State Teachers College, 1939. Education.
Mildred Myrtle Schmidt, B.A., Lawrence College, 1929. Education.
Ralph Norman Schmidt, B.A., Carroll College, 1932. Speech.
Bertha Geraldine Schmitz, B.S. in Education, Northwestern University, 1936. Psychology.
Leo M. Schnur, B.Ed., State Teachers College, River Falls, Wisconsin, 1932. Education.
Effie Tucker Schuster, A.B., Western State Teachers College, 1931. Education.
Alexander Danforth Scott, B.A., Carleton College, 1940. Social Work.
Pauline Fillmore Scott, B.A., State University of Iowa, 1923. Education.
Viola Elizabeth Seebach, B.A., North Central College, 1935. Education.
Margaret Estelle Servine, B.F.A. in Expression, Nebraska Wesleyan University, 1931. Speech.
Earl Smith Shanaberger, B.S., Purdue University, 1932. Education.
Goldie Rosenthal Shapiro, Ph.B., University of Chicago, 1929. Social Work.
Zeena Shapiro, B.S., Battle Creek College, 1935. Social Work.
Waunita Taylor Shaw, B.A., Drake University, 1924. Speech.

[41]

Mabel M. Shelquist, A.B., York College, 1928. Education.
Marjorie Albertine Shepard, A.B., University of Michigan, 1924. Education.
Luther LeRoy Siemers, B.A., University of Illinois, 1935. Speech.
Melvin Ivan Sikkink, B.A., Central College, 1931. Education.
Edward Albert Simmons, B.S., Lewis Institute, 1938. Education.
Joseph Vaclav Simon, B.S., University of Illinois, 1928. Education.
Edmund John Skōronski, B.P.E., Purdue University, 1936. Education.
Wesley Mars Slack, B.S., Sam Houston State Teachers College, 1925. Education.
Bessie Pickett Sloan, B.A., State College of Washington, 1929. Education.
Edith May Smith, A.B., University of Illinois, 1926. Education.
John Emory Smith, B.S. in Education, Northwestern University, 1932. Social Work.
Richard Hays Sneed, B.S., Millsaps College, 1935. Education.
Denton McCoy Snyder, B.Exp., Drake University, 1937. Speech.
Carl Wendell Sodergren, B.A., University of Minnesota, 1921; B.D., Augustana
    Theological Seminary, 1926. Education.
Isadore Solomon, B.S., Nothwestern University, 1921. Education.
Florence Alice Southworth, B.A., Occidental College, 1937. Education.
Agnes Ilo Spangler, B.S. in Education, University of Nebraska, 1932. Education.
William Henry Spears, B.Ed., State Teachers College, La Crosse, Wisconsin, 1933.
    Education.
Frances Lotta Spector, Ph.B., University of Chicago, 1922. English.
Mary Carolyn Spencer, B.A., Monmouth College, 1935. French.
Mildred Arvilla Stackhous, A.B., Nebraska Wesleyan University, 1925. Education.
LeRoy Elmer Stamm, B.S. in Education, Northwestern University, 1939. Education.
Harold Kenneth Stevens, B.A. in Education, Eastern Washington College of Education,
    1938. Speech.
Orva Stine, B.S. in Education, Northwestern University, 1938. Education.
Eric William Stockton, B.A., Northwestern University, 1940. English.
Tekla Wainio Story, B.A., Lake Forest College, 1932. Speech.
Mae Elizabeth Studer, B.A., Lake Forest College, 1935. Education.
Rosemary Suranovic, B.S., University of Illinois, 1931. Education.
Winifred Wilson Swann, A.B., University of Nebraska, 1934. Education.
Charles Moore Swift, B.S. in Economics, University of Pennsylvania, 1935. Mathematics.
Victoria Michniewicz Szubczynski, Ph.B., University of Chicago, 1924. Polish.
Marie Gast Talbot, B.S., Purdue University, 1922. Social Work.
Dorothy Lorraine Taylor, B.Ed., Milwaukee State Teachers College, 1934. Education.
Harold Norman Taylor, B.S. in Education, Northwestern University, 1933. Education.
Howard Teasdale, B.Ed., State Teachers College, Platteville, Wisconsin, 1935.
    Education.
Elizabeth Helen Termeer, A.B., Western State Teachers College, 1932. Education.
Donald Bieri Tescher, B.Ed., Moorhead Teachers College, Minnesota, 1939. Speech.
Donald Thompson, B.S., University of Illinois, 1933; B.Ed., Western Illinois State
    Teachers College, 1936. Education.
Mary Louise Thompson, B.A., State University of Iowa, 1926. Social Work.
Minnie Thompson, B.A., Northland College, 1918. Education.
John Kehl Thorsen, B.S. in Speech, Northwestern University, 1940. Speech.
Irene H. Timko, A.B., Mundelein College, 1934. History.
Florence Ada Tredennick, Ph.B. in Education, University of Chicago, 1932. Education.
Marion E. Treynor, B.A., State University of Iowa, 1924. Social Work.
Annette De Vol Trumbull, A.B., University of Washington, 1939. Social Work.
Donald Richard Tully, B.Ed., State Teachers College, Whitewater, Wisconsin, 1938.
    Education.
John Joseph Twombly, B.Ed., Northern Illinois State Teachers College, 1934.
    Education.
Eugene Merle Vandenberg, S.B., University of Chicago, 1936. Education.
Joan Vander Werf, A.B., Hope College, 1930. Education.
Clara Margaret Van Vleet, A.B., Butler University, 1932. Social Work.
Jean Clapp Vernon, A.B., DePauw University, 1935. Speech.

Evelyn Marie Vogel, B.Ed., Northern Illinois State Teachers College, 1938. Education.
Hildegarde Margarette von Marbod, B.A., The State College of Washington, 1940. Speech.
Dorothy Elizabeth Vrablik, B.S., Northwestern University, 1938. Psychology.
Joan Judith Wagner, B.S., Northwestern University, 1940. Social Work.
Ethel Wiltse Wall, Ph.B., University of Chicago, 1926. Education.
Arthur George Walsdorf, B.Ed., State Teachers College, River Falls, Wisconsin, 1929. Education.
Hazel Lou Audrey Ward, B.A., Dillard University, 1938. Social Work.
Samuel Jesse Wassom, B.A., Iowa State Teachers College, 1932. Education.
Dorcas Louise Weatherby, A.B., University of Nebraska, 1931. Education.
Oliver Cornelius Weaver, Jr., B.A., Birmingham-Southern College, 1935; B.D., Garrett Biblical Institute, 1939. Philosophy.
Claude James Webb, A.B., Ottawa University, 1930. Education.
Janet Tokarsky Weintrob, B.S. in Education, Northwestern University, 1936. Education.
Albert Joshua Weiss, Ph.B., Northwestern University, 1939. Social Work.
Leo J. Wernick, B.S. in Education, Northwestern University, 1938. Education.
Marion Dell Wetzel, B.A., Cornell College, 1940. Mathematics.
Emily Pierrepont White, B.S. in Education, Northwestern University, 1936. Education.
Grace Wiegman, B.A., West Texas State Teachers College, 1932. English.
Joyce Wilhelm, B.A., Morningside College, 1922. Education.
Thelma Chapman Wilkinson, A.B., Illinois College, 1936. Speech.
Dorothy Blakeley Wilson, B.Ed., State Teachers College, Whitewater, Wisconsin. 1936. Education.
Irene Kennedy Winchell, B.A., Northern State Teachers College, 1933. Education.
Irene Rudnick Winn, A.B., University of Chicago, 1929. English.
Marjorie Berniece Witham, A.B., Lake Forest College, 1933. English.
Katheryn Alice Wolcott, B.S. in Education, Northwestern University, 1929. Education.
Willrene Ethelynd Woods, A.B., Washburn College, 1920. Education.
June Bernice Wylie, B.A., University of Illinois, 1929. Education.
Henry Carl Yankow, B.Ed., State Teachers College, Whitewater, Wisconsin, 1939. Education.
Laura Catherine Yargar, A.B., McKendree College, 1931. Speech.
Robert Andrew Young, B.A., North Central College, 1936. Education.
Rose Yunek, B.S. in Education, Northwestern University, 1938. Education.
Melvin Stephen Zaret, B.S., Northwestern University, 1939. Social Work.
Esther Bertha Zarling, Ph.B., University of Wisconsin, 1921. Education.
Harrie Maurice Zeleznick, B.Ed., State Teachers College, Superior, Wisconsin, 1934. Education.
Louis Stephen Zelip, B.Ed., Illinois State Normal University, 1938. Education.
Ruth Margaret Zitzlaff, B.A., DePauw University, 1940. English.

MASTER OF SCIENCE

Ralph Clayton Aye, B.S., Northwestern University, 1940. Zoology.
Joseph Haskell Boutwell, B.S., Wheaton College, 1939. Physiological Chemistry.
Harvey W. Branigar, Jr., B.A., The Principia, 1936. Geography.
Lesley Ernestine Crooks, B.Ed., Eastern Illinois State Teachers College, 1940. Botany.
Beulah Cushman, B.S., Milwaukee Downer College, 1922; M.D., University of Illinois, 1916. Ophthalmology.
Gerrit De Vries, A.B., Calvin College, 1927. Mathematics.
Stevens Stewart Drake, B.S., Northwestern University, 1939. Chemistry.
Edith Brooks Farnsworth, B.S. in Medicine, Northwestern University, 1935; M.D., 1939. Medicine.
Martin Gutmann, A.B., Columbia University, 1939. Physiological Chemistry.
Stanley C. Harris, B.S., Northwestern University, 1938. Physiology and Pharmacology.
Agnes Weir Johnston, B.A., Coe College, 1940. Botany.

Clarence Ray Leininger, Jr., A.B., University of Missouri, 1940. Institute of Neurology.
Lawrence Joseph Linck, Ph.B., Northwestern University, 1938. Psychology.
Irving Eugene Wilfred Olson, B.S., University of Illinois, 1925. Botany.
Harold Markle Piety, B.S. in Electrical Engineering, Armour Institute of Technology, 1923. Mathematics.
Russell n Poppenhager, B.Ed., Western Illinois State Teachers College, 1930. Zoolbgye
Freeman Henry Quimby, B.A., Emmanuel Missionary College, 1938. Zoology.
Samuel Rapoport, B.S.A.S., Lewis Institute, 1936. Mathematics.
Robbie Lou Schneider, B.A., Wellesley College, 1937; M.A., Northwestern University, 1939. Mathematics.
Irving Freiler Stein, Jr., B.A., Dartmouth College, 1939. Physiology and Pharmacology.
William Hayes Whitehead, A.B., Denison University, 1938. Anatomy.

BACHELOR OF ARTS WITH HONORS

Jerome Arthur (as of class of 1940)

BACHELOR OF ARTS

Sidney Oscar Hills
Mary Elizabeth King

Rita-Jean Kucharski

BACHELOR OF SCIENCE WITH HONORS

Edña Constance DeBoer

BACHELOR OF SCIENCE

John Raymond Beem
Estelle Gertrude Blair
Elizabeth Winifred Blodgett
Norman Carl Carlson
Walter Shield Christopher
Juliet Evans
Walter Edward Foley, Jr.
Herbert Gilbert
Robert Edmund Good
Robert John Hammes
Don Edmund Hopkins, Jr.
James Henry Hurford
William Randolph Karsteter
Marvin Robert Katz
Louise Jeanette Kramer
Lulu Benita Krogsgaard

Robert Harris Leler
Manning Earl McAtee
Stiscie Stella Mizenberg
Bertram Bernard Moss
Lloyd Bertram Paskind
Sheldon LeRoy Patten
Frank Joseph Peacock
Halina Julia Przydatek
Jack Donald Rutherford
James Reginald Smith
William Randolph Tenney
Annette Louise Walker
Robert Owens Warnock
Charles Kitchen Waters
James Kenneth Wellman

DOCTOR OF MEDICINE

William Patton Aikin, Jr.
Franklin Longley Ashley
Oliver Austin
Oliver Howard Beahrs
Robert E. Bishop
R. Morton Bolman
Willis Herman Bower
Frank Loron Bracken
John Morrison Brady
Leonard Paul Brodt

Simon Rulin Bruesch
Zephaniah Beall Campbell, Jr.
Harold Woods Christy
Roger Gold Clarke
William Walrath Curtis
Kenneth Laird Day
Roy Fogle Dent, Jr.
John Deetrick Dickie
Edson Fairbrother Fowler
Robert Edward Funk

Robert Judson Graham
David Earle Gray
Fred Sherman Grodins
Roy Edwin Hanford
Roger Ellsworth Henning
Donald E. Hockman
G. Railey Hudson
Ralph Dresser Hunting, Jr.
Archie Austin Imus, Jr.
Lester Earle Johnson
Grant Franklin Kearns
Keith Delmar Larson
Alfred Henry Lawton
John Edmund Maloney
Jean Cynthia Morton
Everett Crockett Moulton, Jr.
Jaroslav F. Neskodny
Manuel Paniagua de la Camara
Fred Ford Parke
George Ford Parke
Robert Joseph Parker

Sterling Glenn Parker
James William Pick
Raymond Charles Pogge
Max Ramirez de Arellano
George Edwin Rathbun
Mary Macgregor Ray
Stephen Emmett Reid
Henry Joseph Rosevear
Norman John Schreiber
John Henry Schroeder
William Bernard See
Paul L. Stuck
Lawrence Terry
Max T. Van Orden
Eugene Livingstone Vickery
Robert White Watson
Herman Saul Wigodsky
Hugh Wilson
Robert Raymond Wright
Wesley Harold Zahl
Bruce Peter Zummo

BACHELOR OF MEDICINE

Henry Lyman Abbott
William George Arbonies
Milton Ernest Baker
Edward William Bank
John Edward Baylor
William Henry Benner
Robert Lee Bradley
John Ross Canterbury
Donald Rossiter Childs
Bernard Willard Coan
John Ballinger Coleman
Theodore Robert Dakin
Thomas James Dillon
Karl Herman Franz, Jr.
Frank Chester Gibson
Robert Pettibone Gilbert
Pablo Munoz Gonzalez
Worth Miller Gross
Robert Merrill Hill
Howard Phillips Hoyt
Don Jay Hunter
George Oakes Jaquith
James Evans Kendrick
Roger Tom Kirkwood
Carl Kline
Harvard Rees Lewis

Henry S. Luke
Carl Harold Lundstrom, Jr.
George Alfred Martin
William Nathan Osborn
James Wight Packard, Jr.
Frederick Moore Peters
Wayne Harold Pitcher
John Edward Promer
Euhlan Luders Rhodes
Burton William Rhuberry
Ralph Dinsmore Ross
Earl Boyce Sanborn
John Gardiner Shellito
Roy Van Sicklin
Richard Clayton Siders
Homer Martin Smathers
Eugene Roy Speirs
Bartholomew John Spence
Carol Listmann Sundberg
Ralph Waldo Taraba
Arabion Nell Taylor
James Allen Turner
Edward Orton Willoughby
Hugh Wilson
Jack Leatherman Wright
Guy Parry Youmans

JURIS DOCTOR

Isadore Benjamin Baer
Robert Winslow Black
Thomas Leonard Clinton
Merle LeRoy Hanson

Daniel Herbert Hanscom
John Jay Hasterock
Edward Henry Hatton
Thomas George Hildebrandt

Robert Edward Kersting
Sidney Jay Matzner
John Joseph Murphy
Richard Phillip Posner

Ross Reid
Leonard Bertrom Sax
Henry Robert Taecker, Jr.

BACHELOR OF LAWS

Raymond Joseph Costello
James Conrad Gumbart
Robert Shannon Hunter

Grace E. Mathison
John Francis Meissner
Frank George Sulewski

BACHELOR OF SCIENCE IN ENGINEERING

Burton Irving Sobel

MASTER OF SCIENCE IN DENTISTRY
With Title of Thesis

Melvin Austin Root, Jr., D.D.S., Northwestern University, 1920. *A Study of Oral Bone, Periapical and Other Tooth Conditions Observed in Routine Adult Dental Radiographic Examination.*

DOCTOR OF DENTAL SURGERY

Donald Thomas Balkema
Stanley John Bartis
Robert Brooks Bowen
George Louis Cermak
Roger Charles Concklin
Ralph Bourne Congletôn
Clifton Orrin Dummétt
George Edwin Ewan
James Eugene Goodfriend
Alfred Paul Jason
Norman Robert Joffee
Forrest Wayne Johnson
Arthur Leslie Kieling
Nathan Kramer

Jerome Justin Manson-Hing
Paul Andrew Moore
Harold Newman
Harry Franklin Pierce, Jr.
Robert John Rowan
Robert M. Scher
Leonard J. St. Angelo
Yiu-Ming Tso
Donald A. Washburn
Walter Arthur Weaver
Allen Thomas Willis
Edwin L. Young
Justin Stanley Zaklikiewicz

MASTER OF MUSIC

Marie Ann Adler
Harold William Alenius
Christine Janice Baker
Harold Vernon Baker
Robert Alanson Biggs
Fred Jacob Bouknight
Howard Franklin Brown
Peter Freeman Burkhalter
Martha Alice Burton
Nadyne Cecile Calvert
Bertha Caspers
Anthony Lawrence Chiuminatto
Arthur Robert Clark
Birchard Coar
Nelrose Isabel Corkill

Hadley Roe Crawford
Mary Alberta Crawford
Wilford Barnes Crawford
William Henry Dale
Isla Marie Davis
William John Strickland Deal
Audrey Beaton Ewell
Elwin Fite
Chester Lee Francis
Dorothy Louise Goddard
William Love Gowdy
Harold Finley Green
Chauncey Laurie Griffith
Isabel Schrage Hendrickson
Vivian Henline

John Lindsey Henning
Wanda Gilbertine Hower
Elizabeth Jeannette Hunker
Alice Manetta Ilsley
Harold McKinley Johnson
James Walton Johnson
Juliaette Holliday Jones
Kenneth Ray Keller
Ralph McVety Kent
Joseph Anthony Lanese
Norma Alice Largura
Aden Kelsey Long
Margaret Ethel Lunn
Vernon Miller
Arnold Richard Nikl
Oscar Emanuel Olson
Mary Louise Pine
Philip William Polley
Adrian Pouliot
Hugh Tedfred Rangeler
William Carroll Rice

Ralph Ritchey
Sister Regina Cecile Ryan
Paul Ryberg
Raymond Albert Samuelson
Alfred Leo Schmied
Ilda Maclay Schriefer
Harry Hadley Schyde
John Michael Sergey
Smith Brinley Shaw
Jane Baker Shedden
Margaret Taylor Shepard
Thomas Isaac Starks
William Lorain Stewart
Kenneth Ray Stilwell
Helen Elizabeth Tanner
Frederick Landy Tooley
Arden Lowell Vance
Cecile Wirth Vogelbaugh
Merton Vernon Welch
Floy Young
Harold Carl Bernard Youngberg

BACHELOR OF MUSIC

David Frederick Geppert
John Tweed Hamilton

Marjory Blanchard Schafer

BACHELOR OF MUSIC EDUCATION

Frederick Eugene Bieler
Betty Eleanor Bridge
Marion Jeanette Davis
Inez Larson

Esther Kearns McCrone
Gertrude Alice Speck
Carol Esther Werth
Dick Orr Wilson

MASTER OF BUSINESS ADMINISTRATION

Dwight Allard, B.A., Colorado State College of Education, 1935.
Elizabeth Anderson, B.S., Winthrop College, 1939.
Phyllis Eleanor Anderson, B.A., College of Puget Sound, 1940.
Ferris Cobb Booth, Jr., B.A., Macalester College, 1940.
Harper White Boyd, Jr., B.A., Beloit College, 1938.
John Newcomb Cole, B.S., De Paul University, 1939.
Donald Wesley Copeland, B.A., Albion College, 1940.
Oral Lee Davis, B.S., University of Illinois, 1940.
Wilbert Frederick Doak, B.S., University of Illinois, 1931.
Ruth Allinson Durham, B.A., De Pauw University, 1940.
Katherine Helen Edwards, B.A., Wellesley College, 1940.
Theodore Carlton Everitt, B.S., University of Wichita, 1940.
Mildred Fall, B.S., Indiana University, 1939.
Albert Elliott Feinberg, B.S. in E.E., Armour Institute of Technology, 1933. *Deprecia-
tion—Its Application to Hydroelectric Plants.*
Alt Feldstern, B.S., Temple University, 1940.
Ruth Heyl Ferris, B.S., Indiana University, 1940.
Elizabeth Foster, B.A., Ohio Wesleyan University, 1940.
†Charles O'Neill Galvin, B.S., Southern Methodist University, 1940. *Percentage De-
pletion of Oil and Gas Wells.*
Ford Rutland Hale, Jr., B.A., Stephen F. Austin State Teachers College, 1939.
Consolidation Procedure Under the Securities and Exchange Commission.
James Hammond, B.A., University of Wichita, 1940.

†*With Distinction.*

Fred Russ Haviland, Jr., B.A., Carleton College, 1938.

Robert Howard Hervig, B.A., Emmanuel Missionary College, 1934. *The Significance of Fixed and Variable Expenses with Reference to Rate Policy in Seventh-Day Adventist Academies and Colleges.*

Rembrandt Clemens Hiller, Jr., B.S., Indiana University, 1940.

Gaylord Irving Indvik, B.S., Iowa State Teachers College, 1938. *Valuation of Closely Held Stock for Income-Tax Purposes.*

Gilbert Stuart Jackson, B.S., Southern Methodist University, 1940.

Ole Simon Johnson, B.A., Jamestown College, 1940.

Adele Juhnke, B.S., Mundelein College, 1935.

Charles Leon Lapp, B.A., Southwest Missouri State Teachers College, 1936. *Effects of Consumer Education on the Housewives of Aurora, Missouri.*

Edwin Joseph Lewis Jr., B.A. University of Western Ontario, 1938. *The Position of the Penalty Surtaxes in the Federal Tax Structure.*

Boyd Joseph Lutz, B.S., West Virginia University, 1937.

Michael Zev Massel, B.A., University of Michigan, 1937.

James Warren McClure, B.S., Ohio University, 1940.

Marvin Davis McMillan, B.Ed., Western Illinois State Teachers College, 1938. *A Recent Financial History of the Chicago and North Western Railway Company.*

Margie Meadows, B.S., Mary Hardin-Baylor College, 1940.

Catherine Marie Metzger, B.S., Winthrop College, 1940.

Albert Carl Michaelis, Jr., B.S., Northwestern University, 1936.

Minnie Caddell Miles, B.S., Mary Hardin- Baylor College, 1936.

Byron Monroe Miller, B.S., Northern State Teachers College, 1936. *An Analysis of Funded Debt with Special Reference to Petroleum Companies Engaged in Refining and Distribution.*

Henry Tsunji Ogawa, B.A., University of Hawaii, 1938. *Accounting Principles and Procedures for Public School Districts.*

Jesse Carroll Paris, B.A., Westminster College, 1936. *A System of Uniform Cost Accounting for Members of the National School Supplies and Equipment Association.*

Martha Gertrude Payne, B.S., University of Missouri, 1940.

Ernest Plambeck, B.S. in C.E., Northwestern University, 1928. *An Analysis of the Applications of the Wagner Labor Act.*

Gerald Alvin Porter, B.Ed., Whitewater State Teachers College, 1936. *Realized and Unrealized Income.*

Margaret Prendergast, B.S., Colorado State College, 1939.

Harry James Prior, B.S., Linfield College, 1940.

John Albert Retzke, B.B.A., University of Toledo, 1940. *Processing Taxes Under the Agricultural Adjustment Act.*

Winifred Marie Robertson, B.S., Boston University, 1940.

Joseph Wilson Rogers, B.S., High Point College, 1937.

John Creath Speer, B.S., University of Mississippi, 1939.

William John Stanton, Jr., B.S., Lewis Institute, 1940.

Paul Richard Sturtz, B.B.A., University of Toledo, 1940. *Simplified Accounting Methods for Small Retail Stores.*

William James Wakefield, B.S., University of Alabama, 1940.

June Elizabeth Weber, B.A., Michigan State College, 1940.

Hanan Wedlan, B.S., Washington University, 1937. *Federal Old-Age Benefits Systems.*

Milton Westhagen, B.S., Northwestern University, 1933. *Obsolescence in Chicago.*

BACHELOR OF SCIENCE IN COMMERCE

Robert Dana Britigan
Clarence Lee Cozad
William Robert Gillies
‡George Jacob Jansen
James Redfield McIntyre

Mary Catherine Meyers
John Charles Podlesak
Harold Foster Thomas
Maurice Joseph Tierney
Earl Eldridge Warner

‡*With Highest Distinction.*

DIPLOMA IN COMMERCE

Fred Philip Albrecht   Herbert Anthony Walter

BACHELOR OF SCIENCE IN SPEECH

Josephine Bangs   Mary Frances Brownlee

MASTER OF SCIENCE IN EDUCATION

John Kay White

BACHELOR OF SCIENCE IN EDUCATION

*Mildred Wilhelmina Anderson
Ruth Marie Bahr
Edward McDowell Baker
Margaret Blanche Barry
Mildred Eleanor Bartlett
*Erna Emma Below
Marion Virginia Bilek
Hilda Winfred Bliss
Vivian Ruth Bontrager
Alma Baumwerk
Betty Jane Brenner
Josephine Bronez
Juanita Swancutt Burdick
Mary Anna Cassels
Mayme Evelyn Christenson
Thomas Colletta
Hazel Cooley
Katherine Cretcher
Carl Wilbert Dahl
Juanita Marie Davidson
Dorothy Leota Davis
*Margaret De Young
*Mary De Young
Robert Fredrick Drew
*Leora Edelman
*Gladys Giles Espeland
Frieda Rosine Fingerhut
Elizabeth Anne Fosse
Vida Chamberlain Franks
Lois Ann Gallimore
Milton Stanley Garfield
Magdalen Ann Gressle

Evelyn Hlavin
Elma Viola, Hockett
Grace Hoyt
*Rose Jenicek
Svea Elizabeth Karlson
Edith Clara Kuntz
Maybelle Beatrice Larson
*Sarah Levin
Dorothea Sarah Lewek
Katherine McKenzie
Stanley Herbert Melby
Patricia Meredith
Emil John Miklas
John La Verne Miller
*Jeannette Klemptner Nelson
Marie Eva Paulson
Harriet White Pierce
Marjorie Marie Piper
Elizabeth Jane Randall
*Muriel Elizabeth Robert
*Alice Marjorie Sanders
*Velma Sandor
Norman Stephen Schreiber
Ethel Seitzinger
*Doris Shulman
Mildred Siverson
Dorothy Roberts Tharp
*Marian Louise Urland
*Alverteen Elizabeth Wadsworth
Olive Wilson
Reba Lucy Wilson
Mary Byrne Thomas

MASTER OF SCIENCE IN JOURNALISM

Alvo Edo Albini, B.A., University of Wisconsin, 1940.
Mason Virgil Blosser, B.A., Bluffton College, 1940.
Paul Mohamed Boutebiba, B.A., Lycee Carnot, 1935; B.A., New York University, 1939.
Jane Alice Hall Cobb, B.A., Texas State College for Women, 1937.
Rodney Fox, B.S., Iowa State College, 1930.
Leroy Wood Furry, B.A., Iowa State Teachers College, 1935.
Irma Goeppinger, B.S., University of Iowa, 1931.

*Work completed through the University College.

[49]

John Jay Haney, B.S., South Dakota State College, 1934.
Olive Benbrook James, B.A., University of Michigan, 1911.
James Douglas Johnson.
Robert Harry Lash.
Marjorie Ann Mayland, B.S. in J., Northwestern University, 1939.
Lawrence Leonard Pike, A.B., University of Nebraska, 1926; M.A., University of Nebraska, 1930.
Robert Willison Schnuck, B.S., Northwestern University, 1940.
John Thomas Trebilcock, A.B., Wayne University, 1935.

BACHELOR OF PHILOSOPHY

Florence Bouzas
Mary Elizabeth Campbell

John Kopcha
Allen Edgar Orr

PRIZES AND HONORS, 1941-42

FLORSHEIM DEBATE PRIZES: Georgia Bayless, Betty Marie Bell, Jane Forester, Mary Ellen Brunenkant, Catherine Hopfinger, Allan Conwill, Donald J. Geiger, Lloyd Klein, Paul Anton Larson, James Julian Rathbun

CUMNOCK DEBATE PRIZES: John Caster, John Forester, James William Knoernschild, Edmund Mizel, Wilson Nicoll

AGNESS LAW DEBATE PRIZES: Madelon Golden, Ruth Helm, Purdie Wanda Nelson, Jackie Lou Reid, Mary Ellen Robinson, Mary Lou Sauer

NORTHERN ORATORICAL LEAGUE LOCAL CONTEST: James Rathbun

KIRK PRIZE FOR EXCELLENCY IN PUBLIC SPEAKING: James Rathbun

HONORS IN PUBLIC SPEAKING: Robert Bohrer, Catherine Hopfinger

CLARION DE WITT HARDY MEDAL: Georgia Bayless, Dwight Croessmann, Catherine Hopfinger

DELTA SIGMA RHO

Betty Marie Bell	Norman Miller
Edward Robertson McHale	James Rathbun

SIGMA XI

Active Membership

Julian L. Azorlosa	Humbert Morris
Donald George Botteron	Bernard Nelson
Dan Youngs Burrill	Gaylord Wareham Ojers
Herman George Canady	Ralph Gottfrid Pearson
William Clark Danforth	Mauricio Rocha e Silva
Charles Franklin Eckert	Leo K. Rochen
Elwood H. Ensor	Milton Julius Schiffrin
Franz Rudolf Götzl	David E. Shoch
David Walter Hamlin	Forrest Eugene Snapp
Louis Richard Krasno	Arden G. Steele
Frank W. Lamb	William Hays Whitehead
Mildred Eunice Manuel	Helmut A. Zander

Associate Membership

John Herman Annegers	Loren Aldro Bryan
Robert K. Bair	Frank Devlin
Donald Church Balfour	Alvin Franklin Dodds
Charles L. Bieber	Oliver Edward Edwards
James E. Birren	Charles Francisco
Carl Ellsworth Black, III	Jesse Norman Frederick
William Andrew Bonner	Sol Louis Garfield
Joseph H. Boutwell, Jr.	Leon Lee Gershbein
Harvey W. Branigar	Wallace R. Giedt

Stanley Cyril Harris
John Howard Huston
Agnes Weir Johnston
Deane F. Kent
Harry J. Kolb
Joseph Eugene Loye, Jr.
Nathan Allen Masor
Margaret McAuley
Edwin William Meyer
Ted Raymond Norton
James Herbert Pomerene
Gustav W. Rapp
Robert Allen Roback

Stephen Philip Ronzheimer
John Shedd Schweppe
Stanley Joseph Skaistis
Leonard Vincent Sloma
Aubrey Arthur Smith
Mortimer Staatz
Paul Richard Stout
William Everett Truce
Ralph H. Wilpolt
James Clinton Winters
Harold Wittcoff
Robert Paul Zelinski
Pari Zia-Walrath

SIGMA XI.RESEARCH PRIZES: Harold H. Scudamore, Joseph Albert Wells

THE COLLEGE OF LIBERAL ARTS

SARGENT PRIZES IN PUBLIC SPEAKING: Richard Pelz, Tilmon Kreiling
CHI OMEGA PRIZE: Charlotte Harris
BONBRIGHT SCHOLARSHIP: Phyllis Ford
JAMES SCHOLARSHIP: Jean Weiss
HONORS IN ENGLISH: Earl Schwass, Frances Webb
DEPARTMENTAL HONORS IN FRENCH: Dorothy Kell
DEPARTMENTAL HONORS IN ITALIAN: Italia Malato
DEPARTMENTAL HONORS IN SPANISH: Lorna MacCallum
DEPARTMENTAL HONORS IN SOCIOLOGY: Hope Quirk

PHI BETA KAPPA

John Corby Andrae
Edna Elizabeth Ash
Jean Bundy Boggs
Kenneth Cleophas
Elizabeth Wilbourn Cobb
Margaret Helen Cox
MacFarland William
    Culbertson II
Mary Jane Fetzer
Phyllis May Ford
Seymour Abraham Fox
Dorothy Jean Fuller
Maxine Louise Gordon
Patricia Jean Grover
Jean Ellen Harper
Charlotte Beatrice Harris
Muriel May Johnson
Jacqueline Kadet
Dorothy Jane Kell
Charlotte Kieferstein
Lois Helen LaCroix
Gordon Ellenby Langlois

Lorna Jean MacCallum
Italia Frances Malato
Randolph Walke-McCandlish, Jr.
Portia Osie McClain
Helen Grace McCullough
Mary Ellen Munger
Alice Elizabeth Nightingale
Mary Avery Ogden
William Marriott Otto
Walter Shoemaker Phares
Catherine Barbara Putnik
Claire Joseph Raeth
Bernard Gordon Rosenthal
Robert John Salvesen
Mary Ellen Sams
Earl Robert Schwass
Ade Louis Shaw, Jr.
Herbert Lazarus Steinberger
Mary Ellen Thompson
James Robertson Ward
Frances Webb

Jean Louise Weiss
Jack Palmer White
Harry Bixler Williams, Jr.

Frank Myron Wright, Jr.
Anne Catherine Zimmer

THE MEDICAL SCHOOL
ALPHA OMEGA ALPHA
Seniors

Alfred I. Shopera
Edward H. Daseler
Philip W. Smith
Milton D. Ratner
David R. Barnum
Robert P. Gilbert

Roland P. Ladenson
Wilford A. Brooksby
Frank T. Padberg
Robert T. Wheeler
Howard P. Hoyt

Juniors

James Roth
J m L. Orbison
George Earle Irwin, Jr.

George Marshall Whitacre
Helen Patton

THE LAW SCHOOL
ORDER OF THE COIF

James A. Rahl
Ross Reid
Stephen Ladd

Howard P. Castle
David M. Gooder
Amy Ruth Mahin

THE SCHOOL OF ENGINEERING
SWIFT SCHOLARSHIP: Aubrey Arthur Smith
SENIOR HONORS AWARD: James Herbert Pomerene

TAU BETA PI
(National Honorary Engineering Fraternity)

Wallace Reid Giedt
Joseph Eugene Love, Jr.
Edward Martin McMillan
James Herbert Pomerene

Stephen Philip Ronzheimer
Stanley Joseph Skaistis
Leonard Vincent Sloma
Aubrey Arthur Smith

THE TECHNOLOGICAL INSTITUTE
JUNIOR HONORS AWARD: George Leon Hitt
SOPHOMORE HONORS AWARD: Roger Alan Burt

THE DENTAL SCHOOL
OMICRON KAPPA UPSILON

John A. Anderson
Lorenz P. Bunker
Walter D. Doering
Marcus C. Funk
Arthur E. Gunderson

Lawrence G. Khedroo
Ricardo Kriebel Rodriguez
Thomas E. Lewis
Clifford K. Lossman
Warren R. Maynes

THE SCHOOL OF MUSIC
Pi Kappa Lambda
(National Honorary Music Fraternity)

Anthony Chiuminatto
Birchard Coar
Hadley Crawford
Mary Crawford
Wilford Crawford
John Creighton
Fred Dempster
Anna-Louise de Ramus
Ruth Ecton
Dorothy Feemster
Chester Francis
Helen Fulghum
David Geppert
Milton Goldberg
Ellen Greenberg
Chauncey Griffith
Sherwood Hall
Claribel Hill
Genevieve Hresiokt
Harry Jacobs

Evonne Jacquart
Richard Johnson
Marguerite Kelly
Patricia King
Ira 'Kipnis
Richard Madden
Kathryn McDonald
Lloyd Norlin
Frances Pryor
William Rice
Amanda Robbins
Sister Regina Cecile Ryan
Alfred Schmied
Arwin Schweig
Margaret Shepard
John Tegnell
Gordon Terwilliger
Frederick Tooley
Cecile Vogelbaugh
Harold Youngberg

THE SCHOOL OF COMMERCE
Beta Gamma Sigma

Evanston Division

Roger Elmer Anderson
Alan Howard Bede
Robert Spence Bohrer
Harper White Boyd
Thomas Peter Conforti
William Francis Drohan, Jr.
David Frumkin
Robert James Gormley
Gaylord Irving Indvik
Leon Lenkoff
John Philip Lindgren

Charles Russell Magel
James Andrew McBride
Marvin Davis McMillan
Donald Richard Moller
Harold Isaac Niemi
Paul Reimer Nutt
Leonard William Pedersen
Sidney Ross
Raymond Wesley Salstrom
Harry D. Simon
John Battista Vottero

Beta Gamma Sigma Scholarship: Donald Richard Moller
Delta Sigma Pi Prize: John Philip Lindgren

Chicago Division

Henry Bauling
Hugh Daniels Jones

Elmer Jessen Scheer

Delta Mu Delta

Marvin Joseph Berger
Richard Crisp
Hugh Daniels Jones
John Charles Newman

Carl Einar Pearson
Edward Theodore Podraza
Roy R. Wixom

JOSEPH SCHAFFNER PRIZE: Carl Einar Pearson
ALPHA KAPPA PSI PRIZE AND MEDALLION: Robert Neuschuler
DELTA SIGMA PI PRIZE: James Alexander Kerr
PHI CHI THETA PRIZE: Florence Marian Unsbee
PHI GAMMA NU PRIZE: Catherine Cook
EPSILON ETA PHI (MINNIE L. PETERSON AWARD): Virginia Rosaltha DeLarme

THE SCHOOL OF SPEECH

LOVEDALE SCHOLARSHIP: Charles Carshon
PHI BETA SCHOLARSHIP: LaRay Martyn
JUNIOR SCHOLARSHIP: Donald Hale
SOPHOMORE SCHOLARSHIP: Wilson Nicoll
EDGEWATER DRAMA CLUB SCHOLARSHIP: Eleanor Erickson
WJJD RADIO SCHOLARSHIP: Vera Bantz
RALPH DENNIS MEDAL FOR SONNET READING: Barbara McCreary
LUCIA MAY WIANT AWARD: Douglas Middlebrook
RADIO HONORS: Charles Carshon, Margaret Haun, Pauline Barofsky
THEATRE HONORS: Acting, William Sweeney and Pauline Barofsky; Children's Theatre, Leila McMillan; Costuming, Ruthmary McDowell; Directing, Barbara Will; Scene Design, Edward Smith
RALPH DENNIS AWARD IN PUBLIC SPEAKING: Georgia Bayless

THE SCHOOL OF EDUCATION

PI LAMBDA THETA

Helen Hill Alven
Mauree Applegate
Faye Axelrood
Esther O. Cleary
Anne Coomer
Jean Doyle
Marian Emerine
Catherine Garlent
Ellen J. Hardy
Frances Harriman
Laverne D. Lenz

Alice May Morrill
Ruth E. Neuffer
Gladys M. Petersen
Monona E. Reeves
Chandos Reid
Elinor Rice
Marjorie Ann Schloss
Marion V. Schmidt
Else Seitzberg
Bernice K. Terry
Helen Van Norden

PHI DELTA KAPPA

Richard Atherton
Lynn Draper
Kenneth Howe
Sol Kasman

Leonard Miner
Eli Samet
Paul Van Zee
Paul Young

THE MEDILL SCHOOL OF JOURNALISM

SIGMA DELTA CHI SCHOLARSHIP AWARDS

Dora Jane Hamblin
Carlin Treat
Raymond Shady

Allan Williams
Robert Goodwin

HARRINGTON MEMORIAL AWARD: Robert Goodwin

DOROTHY CARLYLE AWARD: Dora Jane Hamblin

SIGMA DELTA CHI CITATION FOR ACHIEVEMENT IN JOURNALISM: Raymond Shady

BASTIAN KEY OF SCHOLASTIC ACHIEVEMENT: Dora Jane Hamblin, Carlin Treat

Lightning Source UK Ltd.
Milton Keynes UK
UKHW010759221218
334411UK00004B/165/P

9 780428 659400